Listening
to the Earth

A Spiritual Journey with Nature

D0012536

To my wife Linda

"The man I meet with is not
often so instructive as the
silence he breaks. This stillness,
solitude, wildness of nature is a
kind of thoroughwort, or
boneset, to my intellect. This is
what I go out to seek. It is as if I
always met in those places some
grand, serene, immortal,
infinitely encouraging, though
invisible, companion, and
walked with him."

Henry David Thoreau

Listening to the Earth

A Spiritual Journey with Nature

Robert F. Harrington

Drawings by Lana Bouchard

hancock house

ISBN 0-88839-367-9
Copyright © 1995 Robert F. Harrington

Cataloging in Publication Data
Harrington, Robert F., 1926-
  Listening to the earth
  A spiritual journal with nature

  ISBN 0-88839-367-9

  I. Title

PS8565.A774F67 1995   C814'.54   C95-910147-0
PR9199.3.H37F67 1995

Copy edit: Colin Lamont
Production: Myron Shutty and Tom Pardy

Published simultaneously in Canada and the United States by

HANCOCK HOUSE PUBLISHERS LTD.
19313 Zero Avenue, Surrey, B.C. V4P 1M7
(604) 538-1114   Fax (604) 538-2262

HANCOCK HOUSE PUBLISHERS
1431 Harrison Avenue, Blaine, WA 98230-5005
(604) 538-1114   Fax (604) 538-2262

Contents

1   Are Rocks Alive?

Nelson was tossing a rock from one hand to the other as we walked along a back road near home. From his sober manner, I knew that he was thinking some of the long, long thoughts of youth. Abruptly he came up with the question that had been on his mind.

"Just think of the stories this rock could tell if it was alive, Dad. How do we know for sure that things like rocks aren't alive?"

I don't know how you would handle that sort of question, if a young person asked it of you, but I feel that the serious question of a boy deserves the serious answer of the adult to whom it is addressed. As a matter of fact, we walked along for some time, discussing his question. These are some of the things I tried to bring to his awareness.

"Nelson, that rock is more than it seems to be. Once it was probably part of a mountain. Always, it has been part of a world, part of a universe. It is part of God.

"It is heavy and gives the appearance of being a solid, dense, passive object. Yet, if you could see it magnified millions of times, it would not seem at all that way; for it is composed of incalculable numbers of atoms, each of them displaying constant movement.

"I am not saying that I believe what I say now, Nelson, but, for all we really know, the electrons of the atoms in that rock may be inhabited by creatures as conceited as we are, who feel the whole universe they comprehend, exists solely for their benefit.

"There are many things that we do know about the rock. We can describe it physically and chemically, to a certain extent. We can talk of its properties—its density, color, luster, and so on—but as to any degree of aliveness it may have, or any tales it could tell, we are not given to know more than we can grasp with our minds. Otherwise it is as it was made by its creator, and that he did things according to his own design, is something we finally must accept with faith. All things may rest ultimately on such an assumption as was made by Alexander Pope, namely, 'Whatever is, is right!'

"One awareness you should always keep in mind, Nelson, is that all things are somewhat more than they seem. If the energy in the nuclei of the rock was suddenly and separately released from each nucleus, there would be a violent explosion. It is the same with people—if the hidden energy within the spirits of humans could be tapped and channeled into its highest use, we could almost literally make a paradise of our earth. We could become so good to one another, so kind and considerate, that by doing such—for all we know—we might even rid ourselves of all sickness—even of death.

"There has always been much awareness of the 'power' locked within us. In the Book of Corinthians we read, 'Though I have faith so that I could move mountains, and have not charity, I am nothing.' Such a thought should remind us that passively seeking knowledge and insight is not enough. We must also put it to use in idealistic ways.

"Yes, your rock is more than a rock. It is what you see, and what is known, but beyond that it is also 'mystery.' Some of the greatest men of all time have insisted on the existence of a Divine Mind, for the simple reason that the more we learn about things, the more we become aware of a 'Divine Order' that permeates every particle of nature.

"The poet, Tennyson, wondered about a flower, as you wonder about the rock. The conclusions you can draw are much the same as his, when he wrote:

Flower in the crannied wall,
I pluck you out of the crannies,
I hold you here, root and all, in my hand,
little flower—
But if I could understand
What you are, root and all, and all in all,
I should know what God and man is.

"The rock, or Tennyson's flower in the crannied wall, should teach you a lot of things, Nelson. It should teach you to appreciate what you can know about a thing, but should also teach you never to overestimate the knowledge we actually possess. There is so much we do not know. It should teach you to respect all things of the world you live in—for there are many basic similarities between things even as seemingly different as men and mountains.

"In a deeply 'within' sense, if you try to really understand the wholeness of all things, you will not have to wonder why we should be

8

humble. You will realize that we truly are, as Pope wrote, 'Parts of one Stupendous Whole, whose Body, Nature is, and God the Soul.'

"There is such intricate design and order in the simplest things, that it may indeed be possible that we, as conscious beings, must grow through our experience, until we attain Goodness—possibly it is more than a quirk of our language, that by removing a single 'O' from 'Goodness'—by distilling Goodness so to speak—we attain 'Godness'."

2 Fitting In

One fine afternoon this fall, I roamed for a few miles down a wild river, ending my walk where the river entered a large lake. In truth, my wild river was pretty meek at the time of year I followed it. For the most part, I was able to walk comfortably on sandy or boulder-strewn areas that the river covered during high water. Occasionally I had to backtrack and go around a narrow spot, but such detours were pleasant and offered variety to my walk.

Many years ago, when in the exuberance of youth, I might have made a marathon of the trip and proceeded with undue haste to reach my destination. Now I know better, and I realize that one perceives far more by traveling, and perhaps even by thinking, in a leisurely fashion. One has only to look at the pace of the modern world to know, ten times over, that haste makes waste.

Not being in a hurry, I paused often. After all, every few steps produces another view—another "aspect" of things—and since we are voyagers and guests at the banquet of life, it is appropriate to savor the different sights and flavors that are afforded. Of course, as a guest, one should know better than to gorge oneself. There is an old saying: "One-third of what we eat feeds us, and the other two-thirds feeds the doctor." Upon reflection, you will perhaps agree that this pertains to many things in life, not just to the intake of food.

Pauses are often what make a walk most enjoyable. There was one sunny place where the late October sun bored into a sandy spot along the river. Who could pass such a place without reclining comfortably in the warmth of Old Sol, and looking at the blue skies above? Why it would be an affront to Nature to refuse the hospitality of such luxurious and benign comfort! Things always remind me of other things, and as I rested there, I thought to myself, for some reason, of the brief phrase from "The Ballad of Reading Gaol": "This little tent of blue we prisoners call the sky." I compared the vast blue of the sky, rolling over to the tops of snowy peaks, with the circumscribed bit of sky one might view from the walled jail to which Wilde was referring.

Then there was a narrow stretch of river I encountered, where the current intensified, and bored through a constricted rocky canyon. From about fifteen feet above the current, I could see water hastening its way toward the greater freedom of wider reaches, downstream. I noticed hundreds of floating leaves of aspen poplar being carried down toward the lake. I reflected that the leaves borne along in the current are not too much unlike people in the mainstream of society; subjected, not necessarily willingly, to forces that act with implacable energy upon them.

At this point I began watching the leaves, observing where shifting currents had windrowed dozens of them on the edges of the stream. I looked at leaves being whirled about in eddies and eventually cast ashore; and saw others which had fallen recently into quiet backcurrents, and then washed upstream to be deposited on the shore by tiny wavelets. "I suppose we could call that salvation," I said aloud.

Now leaves are not people, and analogies can be carried only so far. Leaves, after all, particularly discarded ones, could hardly be thought to have free will.

On the other hand, people do have a certain amount of free will, even if it could perhaps be considered a very limited amount. They can ignore their own energy and float helplessly in the currents, or they can use their energy to swim upstream against the currents of our times. By the concerted effort of a thinking society, the entire course of the river of modern life could be changed.

Of course, as I walked on down to the lake, I realized that everything takes effort—even walking. Right now it seems that most human effort is tied up in making money, making war, making whoopee, and in an undue concentration on violence and sex. We would all be better off, methinks, if we just got away from things and wandered around a bit outdoors, in order to let the natural world help reshape our values. If you need some of "the peace that surpasseth understanding," it's out there where the trees and grass are bending in the breeze.

11

3 The Real "Whodunit"

When the moon is filling, and is riding high in the sky, the snow-clad woodland trails are silvered lines wandering through a frosty fairyland. I enjoy an hour's walk at such times. Roaming amid stately trees, I can admire the sparkling snow crystals lighting the trail ahead, or can look upward and see glittering stars marking another trail to an out-yonder that is light-years away. Occasionally I hear a deer bound away, or see one standing like a statue as I walk by. Sometimes a coyote will yap a few times, or an owl hoot will come like a mournful question from the treetops. For the most part though, the walks are quiet and uneventful.

I find that as I walk, thoughts come unbidden, stay for awhile, and move on. Perhaps, like a placid cow with a cud, my mind ruminates, and in so doing makes life's experiences more digestible. Walking, I like to think, is one of the finest synthesizers of experience. Knowing how little we really know, I can find myself fancying that the very stars may be naught but individual ideas in the mind of God; and as they wheel, dip, and cross in their orbits, they too are being synthesized toward some future perfection—a Paradise, I believe it would be called. At any rate, as I sauntered the other night, there came to mind two men I have known. One, a university professor, once told me, more than half-seriously, that he had never married because he had not met anyone he liked better than himself. The other, an administrator, told me he was an atheist because it is not rational to believe in a higher power. In the way that ideas shuffle themselves and line up with one another, as the apples, oranges or lemon symbols do in a slot machine; I found these men side by side in my mind with a third individual about whom I had read—Lord Orrery.

So the story goes, Lord Orrery lived in the north country of England, in the 17th century. Because he had an interest in Kepler's laws of planetary motion, he caused a model solar system to be constructed in his castle. Intricate apparatus was assembled. The center of the model solar system was a brass sun, about which the planets revolved. The complex model included a moon orbiting the earth, and four moons orbiting Jupiter.

It happened that Lord Orrery had an atheistic friend, who visited the castle to see the model solar system. When the atheist asked who constructed the model, Orrery said: "Nobody!" He explained to the atheist that the model solar system "just happened," and had no builder. The friend pointed out the necessity of precise design, and the various gears and wheels controlling the apparatus. Obviously, and indignantly, he insisted that intelligence had been required to construct the system.

As Orrery continued to insist that the whole thing "just happened," the atheist became nearly totally frustrated and enraged. He vehemently demanded that any such product of thought and precise mathematical arrangement, could not exist without creative skill, yet Orrery remained implacable.

We will have to admit that Orrery must have been a master actor; but finally he saw fit to make his point. Orrery said this: "I will offer you a bargain. I will promise to tell you truly who made my little sun and planets down here, as soon as you tell me truly who made the infinitely bigger, more wonderful and more beautiful real sun and planets up there in the heavens."

To say anymore about this subject, should not be necessary. Whether it is "not rational to believe in a Higher Power," or impossible to get beyond the bounds of self-love—well, I'll just leave the ideas with you, and you will make your own judgment.

4 Recreation Has Its Price

This evening I was walking along the road when a pickup truck with a large camper on it plus a boat in tow, stopped alongside in order for the driver to ask directions. We talked for a few minutes about fishing and other things that he was interested in. Then he departed toward Trout Lake, with his landlocked boat bumping dutifully behind.

Such an event perhaps should not cause an individual to wonder about the economic system with which we are strangling ourselves, but it did get my thoughts oriented in that direction. I think that a reasonable estimate of the value of the man's personal caravan, would be at least $50,000. Considering that he had to pay income tax on money earned, he probably had to earn $65,000 or $70,000 in order to provide himself with the truck, camper, boat, and oversized motor that was attached. No doubt there are additional expenses in housing the items, feeding gasoline to the hungry motors, and servicing each unit.

One man's meat is reputed to be another's poison, and very likely he enjoys his paraphernalia. Somehow though, I'm inclined to agree with Mark Twain's observation: "Civilization is a limitless multiplication of unnecessary necessities."

Methinks that if I enjoyed fishing as much as we could assume the aforementioned gentleman does, I would forego the fancy equipment, take at least a year off from work, and sit on a rock alongside my favorite rivers and lakes, with a willow fishing pole in hand, and a grand opportunity to think about life in general. At even $150.00 per day in wages a man could easily afford a year of non-working days as substitute for such a purchase.

Of course, even though I use such an example, I realize life is not as simple as I make it out to be. We have been conditioned to believe that it is neither adequate nor admirable, to merely earn a livelihood. Some unspoken and unprincipled agreement has been silently reached, wherein we measure one another by pretentiousness of dwelling, number of luxuries, and even of superfluities that can be displayed. Austerity of life cannot be accepted as much more than subnormal self-punishment. It can hardly be comprehended as intelligent emancipation of the spirit for more important tasks. Moderating your own personal material expectations actually amounts to "clearing the decks for action." Your own moral fighting trim goes up as the shackles of "things you cease to think you need" lose their hold on a spirit that would be free.

Actually I understand (at least partially) the fellows who bump and thump along the roads with their boats. They are seeking freedom and recreation, while serving as hapless victims of an "economic system." Advertising has convinced them that there is a "proper style" for fishing. They must own this item and that item, so they sell their free lives in order to buy items that keep them from enjoying the freedom they think they are gaining. Instead of floating or meditatively rowing, they guzzle the vintages of the government distilleries while they pollute the waters they would conserve, with waste oil and gasoline from their motors. A peaceful Sunday afternoon on a lake is a thing of the past—for the quietness of the woodland retreats is shattered by the roaring of motors and even the peaceful scene of white boats on a blue lake must now be visualized through the gray haze of gasoline vapors.

Let not sportsmen rise in rage over these thoughts. Not all pollute themselves with poisons while they fish, and not many who do, comprehend that they are victims of a malignant attitude that has grown with the prevailing philosophy that for every single thing a human does, somebody else must be able to make a profit. Before rejecting as inconsequential the idea of the polluting effect of waste fuel from outboard motors, it might be well for sportsmen's associations to look into both the quantity of waste fuel ejected into lakes, and the effect on shoreline marine vegetation.

The fault is ours—simply ours—for believing that the good life can be bought across the counter by the yard, gallon, or pound; the kilo, liter, or meter.

15

5 Straight Ahead

Nelson and I were just coming out of an overgrown logging road, onto the gravel highway running through this area, when the traffic from the ferry went tearing past. From the speed at which the vehicles traveled, and the intent concentration of the drivers, one would assume the annual Galena Bay Speedway was underway. However, it was only typical, as excessive momentum is a characteristic of human desperation.

After the last car went by, Nelson asked me if I had noticed that all the drivers were staring straight ahead, and none had apparently noticed us, although we were only about twenty or so feet from the road. We had just stood quietly waiting, on the edge of the woods, for the traffic to pass. After thinking about things for a few moments, he made a rather penetrating remark for a twelve year old, saying: " A lot of people go through life that way, don't they Dad?—Looking straight ahead, I mean."

It's true, isn't it! A lot of people do go through life looking straight ahead. Of course it is somewhat admirable that drivers should have their attention focused on the road—especially at high speed; but, other than that, many people make their life a single-purpose-quest, rarely taking time to explore those side roads of thought and experience that can be so enriching to human understanding.

Thinking of the subject, I am reminded of such sayings as, "Hitch your wagon to a star"—with its implied consideration that one should set a goal and then be pulled in the direction of that goal, and none other. The goal can be one that is noble by its own nature, or can be as ignoble as the mere pursuit of wealth or fame, simply for the personal glory and satisfaction they produce.

Within my own experience, I have been reminded of the dissatisfactions that can come from a life that has been focused to look along a single channel. Several years ago, I was asked to give a talk on pesticides to a group of doctors who were members of a clinic staff. It was a luncheon meeting, and after the short talk and discussion that followed, I accompanied one of the doctors to a nearby restaurant for another cup of coffee and more general talk. In speaking of the complexity of the subject of pesticides and their implications for health, the doctor spoke of his view that he had been trained primarily as a "technician," and expressed the wish that he had received a more comprehensive sort of education—one that would better enable him to evaluate the many side effects produced on health by our type of society. He also said that his own interest would be in preventive medicine, rather than in the purely remedial medicine that limitations on his time forced him to practice. Other doctors would perhaps not agree with his view, though few would deny that an extremely broad base of understanding is something not commonly provided in the normal academic framework.

Many of us need ask ourselves if we live our own lives as though on a monorail. Are we so locked into an inferior life pattern that we cannot live a superior one? Are we looking straight ahead, taking so many thoughts for tomorrow, that all our todays are surrendered without recognition of the truth that tomorrow may never come? Without living today to a high purpose, how can we even dream that there will be a better purpose tomorrow?

I personally am aware that one should periodically evaluate the goals set for oneself, and see whether they still fit, or whether the maturing spirit has outgrown them, and is now ready for loftier pursuits. It is not enough to whiz through the forest of life without looking to right or left. We need time to see the violets that grow on the shady forest floor, and perhaps even to taste the leaves. I could pun and say there is reason enough for tasting them in that they have a large content of Vitamin A. More than that though, one may perchance find an exhilarating taste and fresh insight—and thereby be off to some greater purpose than the one that was accepted as good enough for yesterday.

6 The Renewal of Spring

People everywhere dream of some miraculous panacea that will heal all of the ills of civilization. Each spring, the formula of the miracle cure is offered for their recognition. Oh no—you will not find it in the shop windows; instead it is offered to your view in every meadow, park and every lawn you pass.

When the snow blanket is drawn away from the land by the warming gaze of the sun, there is revealed a brown carpet of last year's grass. Yet, in just a short while the fields and lawns are cloaked by a lush green carpet, which is not only beautiful to the eye but is of life-sustaining value.

This miracle—this resurrection of lawns and fields from their winter torpor—is not a sudden, magical transformation of "brown field to green field." Indeed not! Closer attention to what has actually happened will show you that the massed green effect is caused by the "renewal" of millions of individual blades of grass.

Humanity has had a long winter—and it continues in the human spirit. In fact, it has dragged on and on to the point whereat there is need for substantial change. There will be no "resurrection" of the human "pasture" until the individuals, the "blades of grass" so to speak, each and singly casts off the winter desolation and grows bravely and sturdily toward "The Light."

"These are mere words," you say; "They make fine talk, but are not practical."

Here I must contend that the individual who feels that way, could well be "dead wrong" and in this instance, "dead wrong" is an apt expression, for not only may the individual be completely wrong, but that individual may be "dead" to the truth. It does not matter that we may be facing the economic collapse of many of our hollowly hallowed, and viciously venerated institutions. What is of great importance is that our present spiritual collapse does not become greater, but that instead, from the collapse of our vain affluence, we "springboard" our way to spiritual renewal. We need to remember that it is not the world that is bad, nor is it humankind. What is bad though, is that humankind has steadfastly been letting itself lose the battle between its "will to do what is good, true and right," and its "weakness to succumb to the easiest, least responsible, and most sensually gratifying way of life."

Thinking of human interaction in general, I am forced to chuckle inwardly, although I'll admit that it is a wry chuckle. It has to do with the last time I was in Calgary. Living as I do, in the backwoods of British Columbia, where there are not many people, it is quite natural to acknowledge anyone I encounter. After all, when you see people at relatively rare intervals, it is almost a reflex to say, "Hello," or whatever one uses for a greeting. Anyway, last time I was in Calgary, I found myself nodding to people in elevators, or smiling at them, or perhaps even commenting on the fact that it was a beautiful, sunny day. Well, I soon found that it must be extremely dangerous for city people to thaw the ice they freeze on their faces every morning. I soon realized that civilization has not really arrived, and it is much lonelier to be in a crowd in a city, than to be off on a mountain top, alone in the wilderness. I wondered then—as I wonder now—how much this more or less inhuman attitude toward one another is at the root of the many hostile acts that take place in society. I wouldn't be surprised if there would be a fifty percent drop in crime rate if people started smiling at one another, and recognizing the simple humanity of their fellows.

We can shrivel our spirits behind walls of rejection that we present to the outside world or we can risk the occasional negative encounter in the outgoing realization that other people for the most part are basically good. Acts of spontaneous friendliness toward one another could lead to a greatly improved social attitude on the part of all. Encrusted ice must be broken before a season of growth can occur. If you, by some chance, are a person who has power or charisma, it might pay to remember that the greater one's talent, the greater is one's "opportunity to serve"—and the real purpose of special attributes is service, not mastery.

Service, kindness, mastery of oneself, and outgoing good will. These are the values we should seek. And, in so doing, we will find the spring returning to earth, the "field" flourishing, and the flowers of life blossoming—and herein, we have the only panacea for the great human sickness.

7 Just a Green Thing

I noticed a number of prince's pine, only partly erect after spending the winter under a heavy burden of snow. With apologies to the plants, I collected enough leaves from several of them to brew a cup of tea, taking care at the same time not to remove so many from any one plant as to damage it beyond repair.

I stood there, looking around for a few minutes, to see what other useful plants might be nearby. In a medicinal sense, there are so many plants of value, and so many more about which little or nothing is known. Few of us realize that Hippocrates, the "Father of Medicine" was also both a herbalist, and an astrologer of note. Those who take the Hippocratic oath might well find a study of his philosophy of considerable interest.

At any rate, Hippocrates pointed out that "Nature is the healer of all disease," and the physician is only the servant of nature. Medical practice for many years, followed closely upon human knowledge of medicinal plants. Then for a while, it swung heavily, even violently, toward chemotherapy based on man-made substances. Now it seems that there is again a wakening interest in plant substances. Plant extracts recently derived, have already been cited as being more effective in cancer therapy, than chemically synthesized substances. It has been noted that plant materials rarely cause the damage to adjacent tissue that may be caused by synthesized substances.

However, I did not start out with the idea in mind of pointing out how much wiser it would be to practice preventive medicine rather than remedial medicine—but it does seem that much of the early knowledge of medicinal plants was oriented toward plants that were useful as tonics, physical conditioners, or as substances that would halt an infirmity before it progressed very far.

Prince's pine is an interesting example of a very common plant long used as a medicinal, and of excellent "pedigree" as verified by modern scientific research. Let's look into its attributes, keeping in mind that it is one of those bright green "things" of negligible height, some four to eight inches (10 to 20 cm) that one more or less tramples underfoot quite unheedingly while walking in moist, shaded woods,— almost anywhere in Canada.

Prince's pine is an evergreen, a holly-like plant, and a member of the wintergreen family. If the name I've given doesn't ring a bell, you may know it as pipsissewa, waxflower, or ground holly. Various North American Indian tribes traditionally used root and leaf, (one or the other, or both) for making teas. They used it as an anodyne (pain-reliever), or as a medicinal tea for rheumatism, tuberculosis, and for relief from genito-urinary disorders such as nephritis, chronic cystitis, and urethritis. A poultice was sometimes made for the relief of rheumatic or arthritic pain. By imitation, the early settlers found it effective, and its use was widespread and common until folk-medicine practice gave way to the specialized fields that medicine has become today.

Looking at these plants in the early April sunshine, I am aware that modern knowledge has unearthed a complexity far greater than their simple appearance suggests. Their leaves are known to contain pectic acid, tannic acid, resin, fatty matter, lignin, starch, sugar, chlorophyll, and a substance called chimaphilin. A recent study of 209 plant species, showed prince's pine in the top ten as an antibacterial agent. Interestingly its effectiveness against Staphylococcus aureus (the famed golden staph), suggests that someone is possibly missing a bet by not using it as a "tea," even though it is such a simple substance as to seem "too" simple in a world where complexity is worshipped for its own sake. We have a habit of overlooking the forest because the trees get in the way.

Living here quietly, I can salute the little prince's pines as good and valuable neighbors. Since "Nature is truly the healer of all diseases," I can enjoy a tea from the leaves as a libation from and to the gods. And, I think, in communing with the plants, while collecting a few leaves, I am communing as well with the greater principle that permeates all nature.

If this introduction to prince's pine is of interest to you, remember that it has thousands of neighboring species, all equally fascinating, all a part of the reality we so largely ignore today.

8 The Source

Sunny Alberta isn't a misnomer, as will be testified by many people who have returned to prairie sunshine from a cloud shrouded mountain vacation. As a matter of fact, most of us, wherever we live, are so used to sunshine that we don't really appreciate it. We have to be staggered by a thought occasionally, to even remotely consider the blessings we are supposed to—but forget to count.

Such a thought was provided by an English philosopher and traveller of the 19th century, who wrote: "Glorious Apollo is the parent of us all. Animal heat is solar heat; a blush is a stray sunbeam; Life is bottled sunshine, and Death the silent footed butler who draws out the cork."

It's quite a thought. Agriculture conscious Alberta is busy packaging sunshine for export all over the globe, and meanwhile they who package the sunshine are themselves packaged sunshine, performing their tasks here on earth.

The sun has been referred to as "the earth's power plant." Its active, controlled nuclear furnace converts some 250 million tons of matter to energy each minute. The energy from this reaction radiates throughout space, and the one two-billionth of this energy received by our planet supports all life on earth. In case you are worried about the tremendous amount of matter converted to energy on the sun, it has been calculated that the sun is so enormous that it will take about 167 billion years before one percent of its weight is lost.

In an age when people have commenced to believe that man is top dog and can improvise technologically at will, it becomes a sobering thought to realize that most of our energy is provided by a strange phenomenon taking place on a solar body some 93 million miles away from us.

The majesty and mystery of sunlight does not stop at this point however. Before sunlight provides energy directly to animals, includ-

ing man, it first must pass through the strange alchemy of photosynthesis. By this process, that means "putting together in the presence of light," green plants produce food that in turn becomes muscle tissue, bone and nerve tissue for so-called higher animals.

By the process of photosynthesis, land plants produce somewhat on the order of 40 billion tons of material per year. Much of the material such as wood and straw is not edible, but the rest of it produces food for the billions of people now living on earth. An interesting and essential by-product of photosynthesis is the production of oxygen, essential for respiration. One wonders what the effect of paving many square miles of land will be on oxygen production, and it is discomforting to realize that some major cities suffer as much as a forty percent reduction of sunlight at times, due specifically to air pollution.

This thought that life is bottled sunshine is worth reflecting upon for a moment. The steak on your table is a bit of that sunshine, as is the salad you enjoy with it. The trout you catch in a mountain stream is a torrent washed package of sunshine, and the song of white-throated sparrows, or the scream of a hawk become another animated burst of sunshine.

We stand here on the soil of this planet, obsessed with our own importance, and frequently lacking the understanding of why we should be humble. If we look skyward at the golden orb that gives us our vitality, perhaps we can understand why the primitive tribes worshipped the sun; and we can go another step further and wonder what started the furnace in the sky that provides our heat and our light, our winds and rains, our flowers and forests and our very life.

9 The Waterfall Imp

A few days ago the temperature was several degrees below freezing, and I was snowshoeing along a mountain stream. The air was clear and sharp, and the bush under its hush of snow was quiet. Such a setting is hardly one in which you would expect to hear lyrical bird song; but I did hear a wild melody that was all the more beautiful perhaps because of the season of the year and the so apparent bravery of a bird who could burst into song under such conditions. I stopped to listen, then moved quietly along the stream and finally saw a slate colored, thrush-sized bird bobbing up and down with stiff-legged motion on an ice-bound rock near the edge of the stream.

The bird of course was a water ouzel, or dipper as it is known more familiarly. Its home is along mountain streams, and those seeing it for the first time as it steps off a rock and walks underwater could be forgiven if they wondered silently whether Mother had spiked the tomato juice that morning, for the dipper is a most unusual bird.

As a matter of interest, one reference book mentions that the dipper flies underwater, inasmuch as the wings are used as well as the legs in enabling the dipper to brace itself as it moves underwater in search of the aquatic insects that make up a large part of its diet.

Trout fishermen know the dipper, and picnickers along mountain streams have likely met this bird, but it is probably not recognized that the dipper is a permanent winter resident of the rocky, turbulent streams that flow down from the mountains. It was the grand old man of the Sierras, John Muir, who first wrote of the fact that the more violent the weather, the more cheerily and enthusiastically the dipper would sing. Furthermore, such melody as is produced is of high order and has been compared to that of the mockingbird. I once heard court-ship song in very early spring about a hundred feet below where a small

26

waterfall plunged into a large pool. The melody was so wild and free that I found myself wishing for all the paraphernalia of tape recorders and parabolic reflectors needed to record such an aria. Later though, I thought that such music, separated from its wild setting—although still beautiful—would lack the quality of the lonely scene in which it takes place.

Occasionally, when along such a stream as forms the habitat of the dipper, a hiker may see one of them fly into a waterfall to what seems suicidal destruction. Therein lies a tale though, for waterfalls usually have an open space behind them and a favorite nesting site is found in the crevices of rock behind the curtain of the waterfall. Its winter song seems like nothing less than an ebullient expression of the wonderful hardiness and adaptiveness of this versatile species. On inspection however, it will be found that the nest is a mossy cup sheltered from the spray, and the infant birds must surely be lulled to reverie by the tinkling cadence of the waterfall.

As a poetic effort by a nonpoet, this perhaps describes the character and personality of the ouzels that I have watched in dozens of mountain streams at all seasons of the year:

Dashing sprite of wintry stream,
Carefree imp of waterfall,
Your effervescence lends a look
Of gayness to each watery nook.
Undaunted by the stormy blast,
You sing as cheerily as ever;
Among the sheets of flowing foam
Your voice proclaims your icy home.

Now dipping, nodding, curtsying,
Like a gentle knight of old;
Now whirring, dashing, kiting,
On some mossy rock alighting.

Bird of brawling, foaming eddy,
Born 'neath rainbow tinted falls:
You scoff the beckoning sunny south,
And hurl your song into Winter's mouth.

10 In Search of Ourselves

Truth is usually so simple that we overlook it. We stumble upon it like a boulder in tall grass, or are momentarily impeded by it, as by a branch in our path that we manage quite easily to step over or otherwise circumvent.

As Caleb Colton once observed: "The interests of society often render it expedient not to utter the whole truth, the interests of science never; for in this field we have much more to fear from the deficiency of truth, than from the abundance."

It is possible that living in the woods is a manner of placing oneself in closer contact with truth. One sees more clearly the fundamental relationship between all things. Awareness grows that the eternal order is extremely intricate; and that much of the glory of technological society is but a momentary impediment to the functioning of natural systems. In attempting to set itself above and beyond nature, the human species has increased its vulnerability. When we read the old poem about the Deacon's wonderful one-horse shay, that was built to last a hundred years and a day, we can perhaps recall that when it went to pieces, the disintegration was total. Many of us are aware that the tinsel civilization we have superimposed on the reality of nature, may possibly be more like that "wonderful one-horse shay," than we care to admit.

Not long ago I shared a few days with a grizzled old-timer. Eighty winters have bowed him somewhat; but his step is still limber, and his eye alert. Dog-eared volumes of classical literature line the shelves of his cabin, and a mind unharassed by the mythical status chase remains

singularly analytic. In our society we have a blasé tendency to write-off such people as senile, but historically the wisdom of the elders has always merited much respect. One day, at lunch, he was assessing the worth of modern mobility, and some of his thoughts are worth noting.

"It used to be," he said, "that when I went to town it was a three-day trip each way. Now I have a road by the end of the lane. I'm not saying that the road isn't a great convenience, and that it isn't pretty nice to be able to be in town in just a couple hours. But, I am saying that for everything we gain, we lose something else.

"With me," he went on, "I don't have the Saint Vitus dance that afflicts most people nowadays. I don't feel that I have to be going somewhere all the time. But, I'll tell you, Bob, that since we've got all this progress, people just can't sit still anymore. Now I'm pretty old, and I'm not saying that everybody should be like me, but I'd still rather saddle up a horse and ride off in the bush, than chase my tail down one of these highways. Lately, it has come to be that people just have to go somewhere. They haven't the faintest idea, often, how much beauty there is just within walking distance of where they live; but they will saddle up these modern four-wheeled broncs and take off clear across the nation, and if they don't know what they are looking for, I'm sure I know—because they are trying to find themselves.

"The good Lord meant them to have legs rather than wheels, but they just don't seem to know the difference.

"I've got a grandson," he continued, "who has hitchhiked across Canada and back—not once but twice. He has seen all of this country that can be seen from a highway; but he's never been over to Ptarmigan Spring against the mountainside, because he can't tolerate the flies and mosquitoes. I guess I'll never understand a chap who is happy going eighty miles an hour in a piece of tin mounted on rubber wheels. He would rather play Russian roulette on wheels than have to swat a few flies away now and then.

"Along with the mobility, we've lost our sense of Home! I've lived in this country for over sixty years, and could be set down almost anywhere within forty or fifty miles in any direction and know pretty well where I was standing. But, the ability to be all over the country within a short time has destroyed our solid identification with the place in which we live; and I just suspect a bit that it's the beginning of the end of a lot of good things when people lose the deep-seated love for the immediate country around where they live."

Sober words these! I'll admit that I hadn't thought about them for a while, until I was in town a short time ago and could look over to the Trans Canada Highway. Indeed it seemed that the whole country was on the move. Remembering what he had said, I too wondered where they were all going, and what they were seeking. It reminded me of the title of the famous book, *Quo Vadis*—that means, "Whither goeth thou?"

Maybe before we "saddle up those four-wheeled broncs" he was talking about, we ought to wonder just a bit about where we are going—or whether, as he claimed, we are just going nowhere in search of ourselves.

11 Progress and Paradox

A few days ago I was standing with a group of people when a rather unusual occurrence took place. Some Oregon juncos, which are quite small birds, suddenly and excitedly took to the air, and in the flash of a moment, one of them was buffeted and killed by a rather small, predatory bird known as a shrike. It was an interesting thing to see, very definitely a natural and common phenomenon.

The reaction of the people was interesting though. One lady expressed to her husband that she was glad their small daughter was not along to see it happen. There were other murmurs about the cruelty of the event, and all such comments seemed rather unusual from a group of people who had perhaps breakfasted on bacon and eggs, and would likely have beef or some other kind of meat for supper.

It brought to my mind that just a few days before, I had read of a report presented to the American Academy of Pediatrics, that stated that the average child will have seen 18,000 people killed on television by the time he or she is fourteen years old. Not only that, but it was pointed out that a pre-kindergarten child spends as much time watching television as a student spends in a classroom during four years at university. Equally interesting was the observation that a high school graduate will have seen 350,000 commercials during his growing years.

I know that I have spent many hours outdoors in what we often refer to as the "world of nature," which reference, by the way, indicates that we spend most of our time in a different sort of world we have contrived for ourselves. I actually see very few tragedies taking place outdoors, in spite of much time spent there. I have seen the odd ground squirrel taken by a hawk, and have witnessed occasional acts of predation among other animals, but, by and large, the outdoor world is

31

so vast and harmonious that one's nerves are not jaded by the continual sensation of tragedy.

There is some evidence for the idea that we may be making ourselves into an entirely different species, just by our departure into a new role of life, which to all intents is self-made. Here is an interesting example of how much a species can change as a result of circumstance.

Nobel Laureate, Theodosius Dobzhansky, in his book, *Mankind Evolving*, pointed out that laboratory rats have lived in artificial environments since sometime in the 1840s. Since then the Norway rat thus reared has become a distinct variety from the wild rats from which it was bred, and is dependent on the protected conditions of the laboratory and the provision of shelter, food, water, and mates. It is questionable whether or not the tame rat could compete under natural conditions. Whereas the laboratory rat is less resistant to stress, disease, and fatigue than its wild counterparts, its sex glands develop earlier and allow greater fertility. However, it has smaller adrenal glands, less active thyroid glands, and a smaller brain. In short, it has adapted to the present conditions of the life it leads.

What he is saying, in short, is that unnatural living has helped develop an animal that is specialized for the unnatural conditions under which it lives. Could there be any relationship between the laboratory rats and people? Dobzhansky thinks so. He goes on to say, "The genetic changes that occurred in the laboratory rat, would, undeniably, make them unable to compete successfully with wild rats in the environment in which the latter normally live. But it does not follow that laboratory rats are decadent and unfit—nor does it follow that the 'welfare state' is making man decadent and unfit—to live in a welfare state."

Perhaps the paradox is more real than we think; or perhaps we need to think about it a bit more. We can accept the idea that by the time a child has reached the age of fourteen, he will have witnessed 18,000 human deaths on television; but at the same time it seems a merciless act of cruelty for a predatory bird to take its dinner by means of the skill it has inherited.

Pass the meat, please!

12 On Swimming Upstream

It is a quiet night here in the forest. The moon is silvering a path down the driveway. The air has the extreme clarity that comes after a rain. The shoulder of the mountain is illuminated by moonlight. The whole pristine setting has a solemn stillness.

A short while ago, I took a walk down a forested path. Then I came in, had a cup of coffee, and listened to a radio news program. It is difficult to reconcile the news (highway carnage, warfare, and political soothsaying) with the peace and stillness of the wooded country. The walk down the trail reminded me that a life away from the mainstream is really an escape into reality, rather than from it. It seems like choice between a muddy, heedless torrent or a quiet, rippling stream wandering amid meadow grasses.

Somewhere, we all know, civilization has run amuck and is playing a deadly game of brinkmanship with increasing fervor. Having fashioned the tools of our own destruction, we play games, perhaps unconsciously, seeking a chance to unleash our most horrific weapons against one another. The poet, T. S. Eliot, once predicted, "This is the way the world ends, not with a bang, but with a WHIMPER." Warfare can provide the bang, or increasing environmental deterioration can produce the whimper. Since our greedy economic monster, like a cancer cell, seeks growth mainly for the sake of growth, only a combination of sanity and humility can provide a life-saving alternative.

In spite of the fact that I live in a somewhat uncommon remoteness, I see a considerable number of people. It has been a long while since I have met anyone who is very happy with the way events are progressing in the world. Many people discuss current happenings, then shrug their shoulders, and express the thought, "It's beyond me!" or "I can't do anything about it." Perhaps one of the most noticeable characteristics of our times, if you will look about closely, is a feeling we are being swept along as helpless victims of an irresistible tide. We have responded to the feeling by an outlook such as, "I'll get my share," or "Might as well enjoy it while it lasts." Man looks fatalistically at what man has done, blames it on God, and buries his head in the sands of self-centeredness and unconcern.

In adopting such attitudes, we all forget that human society is a "whole," that is made up of all the people living on earth. Visualize, if you wish, thousands of fish swimming downstream. It is easier to follow the path of least resistance, and go with the current; and that is the way we find it easiest to live. Note though, there is an occasional fish that swims upstream. It bucks the current, swims harder perhaps, but acts as though it has a purpose. No idle downstream swimming will suffice for it. Somewhere along the line it becomes apparent that it has made an individual decision. Can any of us, individually, fancy that life is so purposeless, that we can do no more than drift with the current?

The analogy may seem too simple—but simplicity is inherent in the universe. Humans may desire to hopelessly overcomplicate life, but truth is always simpler than the fabrications we weave around our endless search for illusory status, and glory beyond our deserving.

We are all part of a most amazing coincidence. We happen to be alive in this very moment, in this very series of happenings now taking place on earth. Hot and Cold Wars, energy crises, social disorder, smog, and labor unrest—all are "Our" problem. All future humanity rests, unborn, upon our individual decisions—that in turn will become our collective decisions. If we choose to act in an inane fashion and end human tenure on earth with a war bang, or a pollution whimper, there may be some "less intelligent" species that will learn to live in harmony with natural laws. Individually, we can no longer dodge our decisions. We have to turn off our TV's and turn on our minds. We have to act with environmental responsibility and with human responsibility, to make a world that is in the image of the best within us, rather than the worst. If the devil is in the saddle, as some claim, we need to kick him in the britches, get him out of the saddle, and let intelligence, tempered by insight and conscience, take over the reins.

Time has moved along, but if the rising moon is to look down upon humankind for many more years, a lot of us will have to start swimming upstream very soon.

13 Melancholy Bug

When we think of such talented occupations as those filled by architects, musicians, carpenters, warriors, weather prophets, herdsmen, undertakers and numerous others, we are apt to believe that these niches in life are distinctly human in character. It might give us pause for reflection to realize that each and every one of these occupational niches is filled by some kinds of insects as well as by people.

As a matter of fact, in this day and age, when we swat them, spray them, screen our windows against them, and otherwise display the attitude that insects are most undesirable—it might just pay to gain a little understanding of these fascinating creatures who may yet inherit the earth.

There are more species of insects than there are plants and animals put together. If you learned the names of twenty-five new insects every day, it would take more than a lifetime to learn the names of all those insects already classified by scientists. The species in some families of insects outnumber the stars that can be seen by the naked eye on a clear night—come to think of it, that is if you live in a place where air pollution permits any stars to be seen at all.

Some scientists go as far as to say that on the basis of species and numbers, we are living in the Age of Insects now.

But, let's not get the idea that it's all that bad. Only a few hundred of the more than 675,000 species of known insects could be classified as enemies of mankind. Many of the others could be called neutral, and some of them would be rated very useful, and on up to essential.

Just think—all the silk in the world, all the honey in the world, and all the shellac in the world comes from insects. The world annually uses more than 60 million pounds of shellac and each pound represents six months work by 150,000 scale insects. Even these important products of the insect world seem insignificant though, in view of the fact that pollination by insects is absolutely essential if many varieties of plants are to survive. An example of this can be found in the New Zealand sheep industry. As sheep do particularly well on such legumes as clover, it's quite natural that clover was planted by New Zealand sheepmen, but the clover could only be grown from seed and could not produce seed until bumblebees were imported in order to fertilize the flowers and thus make sheep growing economical.

In the final analysis, we even have to face the fact that insects have influenced our literature, music and art. Many insects have been used as decorations on coins and stamps, and a considerable amount of art was based on the sacred Egyptian scarab beetle. Music lovers are probably aware that Haydn's, "Toy Symphony" carries the chirping of a cricket throughout its theme, and are also familiar enough with Rimsky-Korsakoff's "Flight of the Bumblebee"—strangely enough Rimsky-Korsakoff's son became an entomologist. Not the least of the many literary efforts in which insects have played a part is Don Marquis' well-known book, *Archy and Mehitabel*, a delightful mixture of humor and philosophical observations made by Archy, an educated cockroach, and Mehitabel, a cat who was supposedly Cleopatra reincarnated.

One of the strange aspects of the insect world, more important than we may realize in these days of insect population control, is that many of the spices in our cupboards are substances that plants have developed as natural insecticides. This may seem all well and good until we stop to realize that plant-eating insects have thus already developed some sort of resistance to insecticides, as well as a genetic tendency to be able to defend themselves against such substances. Unfortunately, the same is not true of predatory insects that feed on the plant-eating insects. Consequently, when poisons are applied, the plant-eating insects manage to make a comeback in numbers, whereas the predatory species are virtually annihilated. All this is perhaps reminiscent of Francis Bacon's words, that to command nature, one must first learn to obey her.

An interesting insight into one scientist's evaluation of the insect's ability to endure is given in the last sentence of Dr. W. J. Holland's classic volume on moths. Dr. Holland said, "When the moon shall have faded out of the sky, and the sun shall shine at noonday a dull cherry-red, and the seas shall be frozen over, and the ice cap shall have crept downward to the Equator from either pole, and no keel shall cut the waters, nor wheels turn in mills, when all cities shall have long been dead and crumbled into dust, and all life shall be on the very last verge of extinction on this globe; then on a bit of lichen, growing out on the bald rocks beside the eternal snows of Panama, shall be seated a tiny insect, preening its antennae in the glow of the worn-out sun, representing the sole survival of animal life on our earth, a melancholy bug."

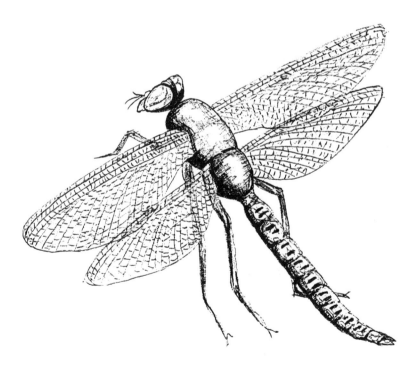

14 Hearing Angels Sing

A mountain is a handy measuring stick. Its very massiveness makes us feel tiny and frail. When one's eye roves up a mountain, over forested slopes of cedar and hemlock, on to still higher slopes of spruce and balsam, then on above timber to rock and barrens, cloaked in ice; a person is impressed with what seems to be the endless endurance of the masses of rock. Perchance though, the eye will stray, and one looks down for a moment and sees a tiny flower on the forest floor. Perhaps it is a bunchberry blossom, or a blossom of wild ginger—and suddenly, one realizes the endless paradox with which nature is riddled. For the mountain, massive though it may be, does not have the force we call "life"—but the blossom at our feet is vibrant with life. One is also reminded of the temporal nature of all things. Flowers are born to cast their fragrance for but a few moments; mountains cast their presence on a landscape for thousands of years—but neither flower nor mountain lasts forever.

Looking around carefully, I see that bunchberries and wild ginger do not always have equal opportunities in life. Some grow in favorable locations, while others grow in deeply shaded spots, or where they are crowded in such a manner that their leaves are overlapped, or pushed at angles by other plants. I search amid the crowded plants particularly, and note that even among them, some of the plants produce beautiful blossoms. I wonder whether their life force—call it determination if you will—could possibly be greater than other plants around them, thus enabling them to produce better or bigger blossoms. We know that there are individual differences among humans—differences in energy, enthusiasm and effort. It seems apparent that there are also such differences among plants.

Once I went afield with a botanist, who was also a student of classical music. In a most inhospitable location on a dry, windswept ridge, we found a lovely alpine flower known as silky phacelia. It stood proudly forth like a brilliant purple flag in a barren desert. I noted my companion studying the flower musingly, and asked him what he was thinking. "Well," he said, "if I had to compare that flower to a human, I would say that it reminds me of George Handel."

"What do you mean?" I inquired.

His answer? "Handel wrote his oratorio, 'Messiah,' with its glorious Hallelujah Chorus, when he was fifty-six years old. He was poor and he was sick. One side of his body was paralyzed. Yet, he must have heard the angels sing, and I would say that this flower must also have heard the angels sing—for just look at the stern environment in which it is growing. People like Handel, and flowers like this one, should be all the proof anyone needs to realize that if the creative urge is heeded, anyone or anything can rise above its neighbors."

It's a strange matter, this web of circumstance, that makes one person a George Handel, overcoming obstacles with might and main; or makes one plant rise as a jewel among flowers in spite of adversity of circumstance. The other night I sat in my kitchen with a neighbor. His roughened hand, curled around the bowl of his pipe, was ample indication of a life of hard work. We were just conversing idly when he looked at me keenly and asked, "Do you realize that all the wisdom of the universe is present in this room tonight?"

I looked at him—a little startled.

"I've often thought," he said, "that we spend too much time reaching outside for knowledge, when it is really within ourselves. Everything there is to know, and everything we need to grow is all within ourselves—we just have to elect to use it."

So, I wonder. Isn't the choice available to everyone, and isn't the matter of becoming a Handel or a glorious flower on a mountain ridge, simply a way of unearthing one's own potential, and applying it with determination?

We are all like flowers on the mountainside. Possibly the name of the slope we are on is "Ignorance." Above us the ridges rise to peaks, and we cannot see the other side—but we know there is another side. Some of us are rooted in fertile places, and others in bleaker, stonier soil. Yet, we have the wisdom of the universe at our beck and call. We can wither before we blossom, or decide not to blossom at all; but on the other hand, we can extend our roots, take a firm grip on the rocks, and raise our blossom to the sun and the breeze.

Should we ever choose to do less?

15 All Flesh Is Grass

About fifty years ago, a tired cedar tree fell across the creek, not far from my house. As cedars go, it was a hefty one—it is perhaps three feet or more in diameter. When I first saw it, it had a tangle of dead limbs projecting from it, like quills from a porcupine. But, I noted it was a good way to cross the creek, and a good place to sit and enjoy the land. So, I took an ax and trimmed off the limbs, and wound up with a natural bridge, as well as a rather durable seat. Seeing that it is a cedar, it will probably still be spanning the creek after I'm gone, and after most of the modern furniture has collapsed, worn out, or been discarded in favor of whatever style is next in vogue.

That cedar log is important to me. If I'm working hard, I can think of the fact that when I'm through, I'll go up there and relax by watching the creek slide by. If I want to think, it's a natural place to go. If I want to look at eternity, I can conceive it better by watching the creek flowing beneath the log—as far as I can determine, it comes endlessly and goes endlessly. Everyone should have such a place as the log over the creek.

A few days ago I was up there, enjoying some sunshine, and the remaining leaves still clinging to the birches and poplars. I was thinking about a combination of two things—one of them was "simplicity" and the other was "how lucky I am."

Actually the two thoughts were pretty much combined in my mind. I was thinking a bit about the simplicity of the setting—the sun, the trees, the creek, the good air—all of these are natural things—"Gifts of the Universe." To be sure, they are exceedingly complex if one analyses them, but they are simple in that they are natural parts of the environment in which we "live and grow, and have our being."

In regard to the matter of luck, I was thinking about the fact that

one is exceedingly lucky when he or she ceases to want many things. For example, I realized that I am lucky in that I sincerely feel no quest for material wealth. What a burden it would be to want to be rich, and thereby have to put one's nose to the grindstone, live on Pompous Heights, and otherwise have to pursue status. Being wealthy would probably impose all sorts of problems such as having to drive a 1999 super Pollution-Mobile, in order that other people might appreciate how wealthy I am. I might even have to wear a pink shirt and a green necktie, or whatever the fashion-lords decree for the moment. I might not even have time to spend sitting on a log, because I'd either be busy making money, having to count it, or dividing it with the income tax people.

The chief matter of luck, I think, is being able to feel somewhat of a oneness with the world, with time, and with eternity. I know that I'm a part of this natural world; not a very important part if I consider it realistically, but a part nonetheless. Being aware of the Law of Conservation of Matter and Energy, I know that my molecules have been around a long while, and probably will be around a long while to come. I am aware of the oneness of all things, and of the flow and interchange between them. Knowing that "all flesh is grass," I can observe the grass, and the soil from which it grows. I can look at the living soil, even at its inert mineral portion, and realize that the potential of life exists even in the mineral grains. We are truly parts of a oneness.

The truth of the matter is that as we shed the complexities of life, we really increase our luck, our happiness, or whatever one would call it. There is a mighty frustration in trying to succeed in a system that is based on sheer nothingness. I hate to imply that such is the case at present, but if one peruses history closely, one might conclude that the most devoted human quest has been conquest. The underlying trouble is that conquest has always been "out there," but never has man learned to concentrate conquest on the most dangerous enemy—his own greed.

Try something sometime. Take a piece of paper, and a pencil, and sit meditatively for a while. Think about what is important to you, and when you decide those things that really matter, put them down on paper. The important thing is to put down only those items that really matter. I doubt that the list will be either long, or concentrated on material things.

16 Packaged Fury

One early November day, I got a sudden yen for a meal of trout, and consequently went a-fishing. In due course I found myself beside a fallen log over a small stream, with one trout on the log and another showing curiosity about a wet fly that I was using as temptation. When my best efforts failed to lure the second fish, I reached back to collect the first one, prior to moving downstream, and almost grabbed a weasel.

From the first it was a stalemate. The weasel wanted the trout, and being a weasel, it wasn't about to accept no for an answer, even though I outweighed it by a matter of at least 500 to one. With ears flattened, tail tip twitching and a not quite comically ferocious growl—for it meant it—the weasel threatened me with all sorts of dire consequences as I picked up the fish—for I had reached for the trout while the weasel was still about two feet away from it.

Now if weasels were the size of collie dogs, or possibly even the size of housecats, I think I might move to town and take an indoor job—because pound for pound, they have a disposition that would make a sabre-toothed tiger seem meek as a grain-fed lamb.

But weasels are not as large as the animals mentioned, and as I said, I had a yen for a meal of trout; so I settled the issue by cleaning the fish and leaving the entrails and head for the weasel. During the proceeding, the weasel alternately advanced and retreated a few inches at a time. possibly sensing that it had at least threatened me into a compromise.

It was the second experience I had with a weasel attempting to sabotage a fishing trip. Once, while fishing a stream up north, I had left some fish behind me on the bank. It was a cool day, and they were under the shade of a small bush. When I glanced at them I was surprised because I saw four, whereas I thought I had caught five. A bit downcast at my mathematical error, I continued fishing, then decided to move along and went to collect my fish—but there were only three! I looked around for the villain, but not a twig was moving, nor a branch stirring. The woods were open for a long distance, with only a fallen log here and there. I sat down on a big rock and watched my three fish, and finally saw a weasel slip out from a crevice under a log and make for the strange manna that had fallen from heaven. Well, I chased that weasel off, and figured that he had taken sufficient tax on my

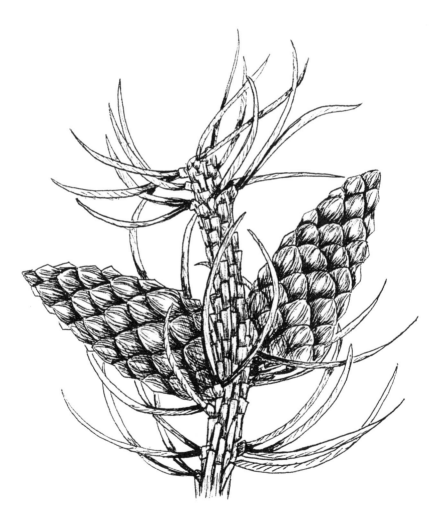

efforts—not that the weasel didn't growl and carry on like a six-ounce demon.

In both cases, the weasels I encountered while fishing were short-tailed weasels. Their adult length, including the four-inch tail, is about twelve inches. There are larger weasels in North America, but short-tailed weasels seem to fill a greater variety of habitats than most of the other species. Like all weasels, short-tailed weasels are extremely slender, and would probably serve well as a mascot to be emulated in the fashionable reducing salons.

As predators they are highly successful, and their temperament is such that they will tackle animals many times their size. They have been known to kill birds as large as turkeys and have no hesitation at attacking a rabbit. Their reputation for blood-thirstiness is well justified, as more than one farmer who has had a weasel in his henhouse can testify.

Nonetheless, as a guest on a farm, they can be extremely valuable. If mice are raising havoc around grain supplies, and a weasel happens to be passing through the neighborhood, the high population of mice will prove an irresistible attraction. Mice will be pursued into the farthest corners, and soon the population of mice will diminish and eventually disappear. Lest we unjustly accuse weasels of depredations in the henhouse, it has been noted many times that a weasel will live on premises with high mouse populations, will quickly reduce the mouse populations and move on without interfering with the orderly life of the hens in any way.

When hunting, weasels are virtually tireless, and myriad tracks after a fresh snowstorm will testify to the endless turning, twisting, bounding and leaping carried on by a single weasel. In spite of their tiny size, a study of their anatomical structure will disclose a formidable array of teeth, worked by a truly massive amount of muscle for so small an animal. Remarkably versatile, the weasel is capable of climbing most trees, is an agile swimmer, and has an almost magical ability to disappear from sight.

In spite of what seems to be an attitude of complete savagery, weasels are known to be admirable parents; and though they are fierce hunters, the talons of hawk and owl frequently seek them out and put an end to their career. It is part of this strange, interwoven fabric of nature that all things have their particular skill and adeptness, but when they become careless for a moment, something equally skillful and adept in some other way is waiting to not so gently remind them that the sin of forgetfulness is not easily forgiven in the world of reality.

17 Finding the Trail

While some look askance upon the philosophy of "doing your own thing," others contend that it is a necessary alternative response that has the goal of self-respect at its root. They contend that it is a way of seeking higher ground in a society that has steadily progressed toward a lowest common denominator in which wealth and materialism have become the focus of life.

The emergence of "doing one's own thing" is not in itself so strange. It is a counter-preoccupation which may have had its beginning many years ago when humanity first started losing recognition of its bond with the earth. When people lost the sensation of letting the fat soil trickle through their fingers; when they lost the feel of the sun on their backs and the breeze in their faces; when years ago they shut themselves up in sweatshops to manufacture products and lead lives regimented by an industrial society; when they walled themselves off from nature in streets that later became canyons between tall buildings—it was then that the human race began diverting its path from the insights which it might, by now have gained.

Possibly the term "desperation" may seem strong, but if you prefer another word to substitute for the conglomerate of neuroses, psychoses, criminality and apathy we are now surrounded with, feel free to choose the one you think most appropriate.

The popularity of the current phrase "do your own thing" is indicative of a new response on the part of a new generation—but it is a generation brought up in the most "automatic" society the world has ever known; yet a well-schooled generation, aware that history has been a continuous tale of human woe, human suffering, and human greed. It is a generation trying to break out of the pattern that history has made, but, having been brought up far away from anything we might think of as a simple life; it cannot find its way out of the maze of human strife to the purer life that it would seek. Perhaps since it has (often admittedly) lost itself, it may fulfill the idea that one cannot find oneself except by first losing oneself. But, if it seeks the lower pathway, rather than the highest pathway, it may stagnate into the negativism that has occupied all the other generations that have lapsed into negativism and passive acceptance of mediocrity.

As always, there are exploiters to capitalize on any new attempt to find reality. If anyone wants to recognize *Vanity Fair* as John Bunyan described it, it may be found in the substitutes that have been offered a generation vainly searching for purity—searching, unfortunately without too much real effort—for something real, honest, and truer than the metallic gold we have substituted for virtue. Disenchanted with an overwhelming system they would change if they knew how; the young stand frustrated, and instead of the truth that costs such a heavy price in self-investment, they may substitute chemical Nirvana in capsule or other form. If there ever was, in Bunyan's words, "A castle called Doubting Castle, the owner whereof was Giant Despair," it is in the doubting young woman or young man who tries to substitute a dream world of narcotics, or alcohol, for the ideal world he or she would construct.

Once committed to a truly worthwhile ideal, the highest goal of life can truly be in "doing your own thing." The really great things the world has experienced have been done by people behaving in just such a manner. The question is, "How?"

The answer is ages old. It involves recognition of the highest quality of human nature. It involves self-purification, but not by means of any synthetic chemicals that are no more a panacea than is a bullet in the brain. Self-purification must literally be by means of self-effort. You face the dragon within yourself, and you overcome it. As Leo Tolstoy wrote: "Our life can have no other meaning than the fulfillment, at any moment, of what is wanted from us by the power that sent us into life and gave us in this life one sure guide—Our Rational Consciousness."

No group consciousness! No substitute at all for doing your own personal thing is possible. Perhaps you will not agree with Tolstoy's conclusions on this matter, but even if you are totally cynical about anything greater than yourself, it will not hurt you to reflect on these words with which he concluded one of his most famous books:

"The only meaning of man's life consists in serving the world by cooperating in the establishment of the kingdom of God; but this service can be rendered only through the recognition of the truth, and the profession of it, by every single individual. The kingdom of God cometh not with observation; neither shall they say, Lo here! or, Lo there! for, behold, the kingdom of God is within you."

Note that Tolstoy proclaims no one creed as being more right than any other. It is up to you—the separate individual—to do your own thing—but to do the highest thing of which you are capable.

That's what "doing your own thing" should be all about—and we have to recognize that basic, rock-solid truth.

18 Masterpieces

Some people were here the other day, and were talking to one another in a somewhat learned fashion about art, music, and literature. They seemed to be pretty much self-starting and self-perpetuating, so I didn't have to involve myself very much.

I don't want to decry any of the subjects mentioned: art, music, or literature. It's just that while they were talking, my mind was roaming.

For example, they were talking about great masterpieces—and while they were discussing famous painters, I couldn't help but think of one of the great masterpieces that I sat in the middle of—with reverence. It was a northern lake up in the Ootsa country of British Columbia. The sun was setting behind Mount Wells, which is known as "The Dome." Long shadows of trees were reaching fingerlike out into the lake that was partly darkened, and partly still in mellow light. Loons were laughing riotously on the lake; fox sparrows were singing sleepily in the willow brush along the shore. I was reclining in front of the glowing coals of a small campfire; and to give the masterpiece a living touch of the Great Artist, a bull moose was standing across the lake in shallow water. A bit earlier he had been feeding on rushes or sedges; but in the dying moments of the day, he was immobile as a statue, and remained thus until he disappeared in the gathering twilight across the lake. As the people talked, such was my vision, and I couldn't help but think that it is nicer to live in a masterpiece, than to merely go to an art gallery occasionally to view one hanging on a wall.

They continued talking, and began discussing symphonies. I could still hear that ringing laughter of the loons in my mind. I could call back to memory the sound of little waves lapping on the shore, the sound of the wings of a flock of ducks whistling as they circled the lake to land for the night, and the sound of an occasional frog making a solemn pronouncement very reminiscent of someone calling for a "Jug-O-Rum." Faint whispers of breeze served as tremolo, and the slap of a rainbow trout leaping from, and falling back into the water was significant percussion. Much as I might enjoy the occasional bit of symphonic music, I think I am firmly committed to the art and music of nature.

They were happy in their discussion of art and music, so I didn't really feel it appropriate to disturb their sort of "stamp collecting approach" to the general topic. But it did remind me that Alexander Pope had once written something about the subject, and I later went to look up his thoughts. In the "Essay on Man," he observed, "All nature is but Art, unknown to thee," and in his "Essay on Criticism" he elaborated as follows:

First follow Nature, and your judgment frame
By her just standard, which is still the same;
Unerring Nature, still divinely bright,
One clear, unchanged, and universal light;
Life, force, and beauty must to all impart,
At once the source, and end, the test of art.

I am content that the great men of art have indeed created masterpieces. Yet, it makes me chuckle a bit ruefully, that a painting such as the Mona Lisa is worth millions of dollars; whereas in our economic slaughterhouse, we cannot see millions of dollars worth of art and grace—and life—in a beautiful stand of fir or hemlock. We insure the oil paintings on canvas but rip and rend asunder the great art of the Greatest Artist, with relentless bulldozers. What company will insure a landscape from the profiteers? Isn't it strange that one would need a Ph.D. to teach basket-weaving in a university, but no particular education is needed to operate a massive piece of earth-moving equipment? I would think that a person operating such equipment would need the equivalent of a half-dozen or so Ph.D.s.

Who can make a painting like a glorious sunset over the Rockies? Who can duplicate the charm of the northern lake I mentioned? What brush can depict the grace of a swallow-tail butterfly in flight, or the rocketing leaps of a startled mule deer? What madrigal equals in sweetness the pensive notes of a thrush from a darkening spruce woodland; and what composer has caught the rapping of a woodpecker on a dead limb, or the percussive effect of a drumming ruffed grouse?

I ponder! How few realize the art—the music—that we destroy daily as we blindly forge ahead with our senseless destruction of the one really great masterpiece—the earth.

19 Pondering

It was one of those warm spring Sundays. I roamed along an abandoned backroad. The sun was sending a shaft of warmth along the road, through the aisle between the trees. The heat on my back was like a benediction. Varied thrushes were singing, an occasional robin chortled, and a winter-wren was sending forth that rippling melody so typical of a woodland spring.

Before reaching the place where I was strolling, I had walked about a mile on the main highway. A ferry had recently docked and a series of a half dozen or more small cars went racing by—out for a Sunday drive I suppose, going nowhere in particular, because the road really doesn't lead to any large town. From past observation, I knew that the same cars would be tearing back in the opposite direction an hour or two later—the Sunday drive being some sort of race with oneself in which one went as far as possible in a given direction and length of time, and then hastened madly back in a homeward direction.

How can they stand it, I wondered? Here it is a beautiful spring day; we have bodies that were meant to walk and be active in the sun. We have senses that can perceive things at walking speeds. Have we become so enslaved to machines—dehumanized—that in truth we are obediently taking the machines for their Sunday airing?—while we get none for ourselves? When did we cease making machines for our convenience, and when did they take us over and start us on the path of reproducing them for their own pleasure? Look at North America— paved from one end to the other, with new roads ever being sought! Certainly very few people get out and walk any distance now, nor do many people use machines to a minimum extent in order to gain a maximum benefit for themselves. Consider it well: we are changing the whole face of the earth for the sake of machines. We destroy peoples'

51

homes and farms, because at all human costs, highways must go through, so that the machines can be on time in their journey from nowhere to nowhere. We uproot forests, blast mountains, and fill ponds—nothing is sacred, no beauty is spared before the onslaught of the machine.

Almost all of us spend too much time evading the true price we are paying for counterfeit convenience. How can we avoid thinking, at least occasionally of "How the Mighty have Fallen?" Why is it we never assess how glorious humanity, the masterpiece of creation (you say?), has reduced itself to becoming a cog in its own hungry assembly lines? Depersonalization, despiritualization, and dehumanization have all followed in the wake of our willing enslavement to anything that goes "puff, snort or rattle." We have been seduced by the myth of the machine, hypnotized by the hum of power. If we spent half the care on our bodies that we spend on our machines, the hospitals would probably be less than half as full—at least they wouldn't be full of traffic victims.

I found a dry log—one that had been in the sun enough for the residual moisture from the winter snow to be baked out of it. I opened my knapsack and took out a sandwich, a thermos of coffee, and an apple. Such tremendous wealth I thought, and all those poor, poor people in their ugly machines. Yes, I know (I reminded myself), they don't think they are poor, and certainly some of them would feel I am an idiot for expressing these sentiments, but think of all the things they don't realize—about bird song and the pleasure of hearing it, about the warmth of the sun, the pleasure of walking, the pleasant smell of the cool woods, about the lazy enjoyment of just being a sort of outdoor animal and absorbing the smells, sights and sounds of a wonderful Creation. Ha! There goes a toad hopping along—I'll bet he's glad it's spring—and how sad it is to walk along roads and see the countless small animals, like that toad, crushed beneath the wheels of these shrieking demons that have become lords and masters of not only the highways, but of the very hearts of men and women.

Now there's the first mosquito I've seen this season—one of those early, big ones we call snow mosquitoes. They rarely seem to be interested in bothering a person though—too sluggish I guess. It's still pretty cool for a mosquito to be really active. And there's a mourning-cloak butterfly—that's one of the species that hibernates and lives through the winter—he or she is a pretty bedraggled looking individual, but I guess that once reproduction has been carried on, its purpose on earth is about over.

Yes, I mused from my vantage point on that comfortable log, I understand exactly what Thoreau meant when he said that he would rather "sit alone on a pumpkin than be crowded on a velvet cushion." He knew that a person was better off seeking quietly to understand the harmony of nature and the music of the spheres, than to chase an ulcer from one corner of the country to another.

Seriously—try it some day! Just take a walk, and a lunch, and find a log and sit and be part of it all for a while. It's a good earth you realize, a real gift from heaven, and it's a shame we don't enjoy it more as it is, and stop wrecking it just so that the machine society that is replacing humanity can take it over.

20 Cupboard Thoughts

In this day of supermarkets and handy transportation, the problem of food storage is of almost negligible concern for the individual. A minority of us who still live in a rural setting are apt to have a few weeks food supply on hand, but for most of us, groceries are only minutes away.

Other mammals don't have things quite so easy, and this winter's comfort may depend to a large measure on their success in foraging and storing food during the summer months. A variety of interesting habits are involved as different mammals go about the serious business of securing a guaranteed supply of nutrition.

Anyone who has seen red squirrels working over the cones of evergreens is probably aware that these frisky animals store food for winter use. Cones may be stored in a dry snag or buried in the earth. Back east in oak country, their grey-squirrel cousins store vast quantities of acorns. As a matter of fact, grey squirrels are well known as uphill planters of oak trees. Since acorns are rounded and too heavy to be carried by winds, squirrels, by packing off acorns and forgetting where some of them are buried, help extend oak trees uphill on steep slopes.

Along mountain slopes, the pika, that resembles a miniature rabbit and lives in rock slides, spends its summer harvesting grasses and other plants, which it spreads on sunny rocks to dry. Later, this hay is carried down below the surface to their dens. Secure from wintry blasts, the pika munches hay and thinks whatever thoughts run through pikas' minds. Cozy, on a dry shelf in a beaver lodge, a wintering beaver who has done its summer homework has only to swim out through an underwater entrance and collect branches stuck into the bottom of its pond. The bark of these provides winter food, and regular attention to the dam on the pond guarantees that the winter food supply will be protected in the reasonably safe environment in which the beaver lives. Mountain beaver sometimes cut bracken fern, dry it, and take it into the burrow.

Other animals, such as ground squirrels, jumping mice, bears, and some bats, store food in their own bodies and in order to conserve energy, sleep away the snowy months. These hibernating animals fall into two groups; high-temperature hibernators, such as bears and raccoons that are shallow sleepers; and low-temperature hibernators, such as ground squirrels, marmots, and woodchucks that are deep sleepers. The Columbian ground squirrel, that, when active, has a body temperature of 98.5 degrees Fahrenheit (36°C), may have its body temperature reduced to as low as 46 degrees Fahrenheit (8°C) during hibernation. Its normal breathing rate of 100 to 200 breaths per minute may drop as low as ten breaths per minute, and heartbeat drops from a normal rate of 300 per minute to about fifteen. During the long winter months, hibernating animals may lose up to 40 percent of their fattened fall weight. Strange that no reducing salon has yet tried to introduce hibernation for the overweight.

For the farmer to look with satisfaction at the spuds, carrots, and squash in the basement or root house is perhaps an impulse older then we know. Possibly the reason people collect knickknacks nowadays is that the supermarket is too near and the chipmunk in us makes it necessary to collect something—even if it's not food!

21 Ignoring History

Sometimes one wonders if humanity learns very much from history. Back in 450 B.C., there was a historian, Thucydides, who wrote a *History of the Peloponnesian War*. In it, he explained that war was not made on people alone, but war was made on the land as well. A typical example may be taken from Volume One of the history in which Thucydides describes a battle between the Lacedaemonians and Megaria: "The battle took place at Tangara in Boetia, and in it the Lacedaemonians and their allies were victorious, and there was much slaughter on both sides. The Lacedaemonians then entered the Megarian territory, cut down the trees, and went home..."

From the cutting of trees, to loss of soil downslope was a matter only of time. Plato traced the history of human impact on Greece, when he explained in *Critias* that the productive soil had been carried away. As he wrote, "What now remains compared with what then existed is like the skeleton of a sick man, all the fat and soft earth having wasted away, and only the bare framework of the land being left....there are some mountains which now have nothing but food for bees, but they had trees not a very long time ago."

About 300 B.C., Theophrastus described Syria as it was at that time, saying: "In Syria and on its mountains the cedars grow to a surprising height and thickness; they are sometimes so large that three men cannot embrace the tree." Compare his description to that of Walter Lowdermilk's comment about Syria in a Smithsonian Institute publication of 1943: "Here are ruins of villages, market towns resting on the skeleton rock of limestone hills, from which 3 to 6 feet of soil have been swept off....the cities will remain dead forever, because their soils are gone beyond hope of restoration."

In the Bible, Moses described Palestine in the Book of Deuteronomy as, "A good land, a land of brooks of water, of fountains and springs, flowing forth in valleys and hills; a land of wheat and barley, of vines and fig trees and pomegranates, a land of olive trees and honey, a land in which you will eat bread without scarcity, in which you will lack nothing."

But men came, and logged, and fought, and scorched the earth, and a modern description by Lowdermilk reads: "The 'Promised Land', which 3000 years ago was 'flowing with milk and honey' has been so devastated by soil erosion that the soils have been swept off fully half the area of the hill lands....accelerated runoff from barren slopes continues to cut gullies through the alluvial valleys and to carry erosional debris out to choke up the channels of streams flowing through the coastal plains."

Have we changed so much? In July 1973, zoologist E. W. Pfeiffer visited northern South Vietnam, describing and photographing a land littered with bomb craters, some as much as 100 feet in diameter and 60 feet deep (30 m wide by 18.5 m deep). His South Vietnamese hosts called the ones that were re-vegetated "Johnson Craters," and the more recent, bare craters "Nixon Craters." Considering these craters, and the extensive use of herbicides and Rome plows in Vietnam, one is reminded of the deeds of Genghis Khan. According to Sir Percy Sykes' *A History of Afghanistan*, when Genghis captured the city of Bamian, his behaviour toward the land, as well as the people, was merciless. "To avenge the death of one of his grandsons, Genghis destroyed every living creature, including animals and plants, and the site remained desolate for a century. So vicious was his war on land that the city of Herat, destroyed in AD 1226, still presents visible evidence of the devastation more than 700 years later."

Have we learned? If so, where are the bison that thundered on the prairies? Where are the passenger pigeons that darkened the skies? Where are lush valleys drowned behind power dams? Where are millions of tons of fat, lush topsoil, blown or washed off North American lands? Why do acid-stained streams run from coal-gutted mountains? Why is acid rainfall downwind from smelters killing fish in lakes?

In the first century A.D., the Roman, Pliny, chided at mankind for digging mines in the "entrails of the earth" for the mere sake of a "jewel to wear on a finger." We still seem to prefer gaudy trinkets to healthy land.

Egypt experiences reduced harvests in the once lush Nile valley, that no longer receives an annual increment of fertilizing silt due to the Aswan dam. Mesopotamia supports a fragment of the people who once

lived amidst the bounty of nature in the one-time rich, Tigris-Euphrates valley. Children in once soil-rich Greece, dig soil from rock-crevices to put on their fields. Here we log steep forest slopes and complacently contemplate fattening bank accounts while the life blood of the land, the soil, is carried away in spring freshets. We ignore history, while it is repeating itself before our eyes. Thoreau once commented, "Thank God, they can't cut down the clouds." No doubt removing all the trees will produce the same effect.

What a hollow thing it will be—to worship affluence, when the land is gone! What a vast oversight not to realize that health and real wealth both have their roots in the earth.

22 You Rang?

Man likes to think of himself as a superior sort of animal—that is, presuming that he will admit that he is an animal at all. Some scholars indicate that our complex language and varying means of communication are an indication of the higher civilization in which we live. Interestingly enough, many of our means of communication are not unique to humans.

Knocking on a door is a means of communication. It says, "Someone is outside and wishes to be recognized." Knocking or stamping is a common means of communication with other animals as well. One way of telling whether an abandoned cabin or barn is occupied by a bushy-tailed woodrat, better known as a pack rat, is to rap sharply on the building: "Knock, (pause) Knock-Knock." The chances are that if a pack rat is at home, he will knock right back in a similar manner. It is characteristic of the pack rat that he will knock with his hind feet, whereas, if you don't mind the comparison, you would use your front feet—all right—hands if you prefer.

If someday you chance to meet a black and white wood-pussy, of the variety called "skunk," and, if he should appear a bit irritated and stamp his front feet, he is telling you something. You probably already understand what the message is, but if you insist on finding out, just continue to advance toward the skunk. Hopefully you will have a can of tomato juice in your knapsack, as it is supposedly somewhat effective in removing the lingering odor for which the skunk is famed.

Squirrels are a very vocal animal and if you spend a bit of time listening to them, you will recognize that varying situations bring about a difference in the sounds they make. Hunters know all too well, that squirrels give alarm signals that are picked up by other squirrels,

so that one's progress through the bush may be announced by a series of squirrels alerting their neighbors.

At least some examples of other animal language are familiar to us all. The joyful barking of a dog, happy to see its master, or the warning growl of a watchdog are sounds familiar to us in our daily life. Less common sounds of communication are the slapping of a beaver tail on a quiet pond, warning of an intruder, or the bugling of a bull elk in the fall announcing to all other elk that a lordly warrior is on the move. Animal language goes considerably farther still. Anyone who has seen a white-tailed deer raise the glistening flag of its tail, knows that this is visual communication to other deer. It plainly announces the fact that the deer is alarmed, and frequently is followed by the graceful stalking gait often adopted by deer retreating to safer cover. In a similar manner, twin white patches, one on each buttock of an antelope, are erected by a subdermal circular muscle that causes the patches to flash like a heliograph, thus serving to announce danger to other members of the species.

Facial grimaces in dogs may be studied to detect attitudes held by the dog, and the upcurled lips and bared fangs of a threatening dog need hardly be read about to be understood. Those relatively unfamiliar with dogs might misunderstand the "grinning" of a sheepish dog as threatening, but observation will tell you that the whole posture of the dog is different when such an expression occurs.

Animal scents are used to mark boundaries of territories and to announce their presence to other animals. Humanity's inability to cash in on scent messages may be one of the prices of the higher civilization we now enjoy. Our poor sense of smell has served to make us less alert to what is about us when we stroll through wooded areas.

As a concluding example of animal communication, those who travel afoot in bear country occasionally come across trees used as signposts by bears. Claw marks are used as signatures, and the higher a bear can reach from the ground to claw the tree, the higher will be the signature that he or she leaves on the tree. Human muscle-flexing, posturing or modeling are not really unique ways of saying, "Hey buddy, I'm big, tough, or pretty—so pay attention, or admire me," or whatever the case may be.

As William Cullen Bryant wrote in the poem, "Thanatopsis:"
To him who in the love of Nature holds
Communion with her visible forms, she speaks
A various language.

23 Storm

The other afternoon I worked in the garden for an hour or two. After a while, I noted that the sun had gone, the mosquitoes and black flies were taking on the persistent attitude they usually adopt before a storm, and thunderclouds were massing over the mountains.

Somehow the approaching storm "felt" a bit more ominous than most do. There was a brooding quietness in the air, with none of the low rumbling sounds of thunder that often precede a storm.

I finished my work and then picked some lettuce, chives, swiss chard leaves, and radishes to make myself a salad. I also picked a few leaves to add to the salad from a fireweed plant growing nearby, and then found a few wild onions in the woodland edge. With a view to dessert, I gathered fifteen or twenty strawberries and took my provender into the house.

In due time I was enjoying supper and a good book at the same time. When I got up to pour myself a cup of coffee, I noticed that it was both unnaturally still outside, and unnaturally dark—for 5:30 P.M. I heard a breeze start up a few minutes later and noticed the tree tops beginning to dance a bit; but I wasn't prepared for a sudden deafening peal of thunder, drumming rain on the roof, and the sound of rapidly rising wind. In just a few moments the trees were beginning to lean strongly from the wind, and through the open window I could hear the sound of an occasional dead tree crashing to the ground.

I began to contemplate the fact that there are many trees within a short distance of the house. A tree seventy feet high, and sixteen to seventeen inches (40 to 43 cm) in diameter at ground level—standing only about thirty-five feet (11 m) from the house—can constitute an interesting problem of mathematical probability for damage to a house when winds begin to blow willy-nilly and seemingly from all directions at once. However, realizing deeply inside myself, that all such things are in the hands of the impartial forces of nature—and that I could do nothing about it—I wandered around the house, looking through the various windows in order to enjoy the impressive savagery of the storm. One can always build or repair a shelter if need be, so there really isn't much point in doing anything other than enjoying such a spectacle.

Before my eyes, a tall poplar broke off at about midheight and toppled over, still attached at the breaking point, to form an inverted V. I thought to myself that it wasn't going to make the best firewood, but I would have to clean it up anyway. Next was a hemlock that fell across the driveway, and then another candidate for the saw made application in the form of a cedar that adopted a permanent forty-five degree lean, without actually falling.

And so it went, until the storm finally abated. The heavy snow pack still on the mountains, plus the heat of the day, had, I suppose, made possible the generation of such a wind. About another half hour, and another cup of coffee passed, and then the sun was shining as beneficently as though the spirits of the wind had not been indulging in a momentary mad caprice.

The dog had been very quiet during the storm—laying there on her rug somewhat tensely, wondering perhaps at what was going on outside. But now, she was ready and raring to go—so we went out for a walk just to see how the world looked. When I gazed over the bank toward the road, I was greeted with the sight of another half dozen trees down, and realized that I had quite a bit of work ahead of me turning them into firewood.

But—the thing I noted as we ambled along the road, was not the damage of the storm so much as the beauty and serenity that came after the storm. It seemed as though every bird was madly singing in an effort to reassure the living world that the aftermath of any storm should be joy. The sun was making diamonds of millions of raindrops still clinging to the foliage. The air was clean and fragrant. The dog sniffed here and there excitedly, with tail wagging. Every few minutes she came bounding spontaneously and joyfully to me.

A storm had raged, and had done its damage indeed. But storms are a part of life experience—probably as necessary in individual, personal lives as they are in the rest of the natural world. In their abatement they provide new room for growth, new opportunities for joy and appreciation. Like the trees with well-anchored roots and resilient stems, it pays to arrange your life and thought to hang on that extra moment until the storm is over—and the birds sing—and the message of new, abundant joy resounds throughout the world.

24 Tillers of the Soil

A single acre of prairie land exposes five to ten acres of leaf surface to the sun. Truly the prairies are the breadbaskets of nations.

Once, of course, the prairies were the breadbaskets of countless animals other than man. Elk ranged on the prairies, antelope, bison, coyotes and wolves made the prairie world alive. The lumbering grizzly ranged onto the prairie before the fear of man caused this animal to retire to the mountain sanctuaries. Even before the day of the white man, there were towns on the prairie, and it is these towns, prairie dog towns, which we will look into for a moment.

The prairie dog has been known by many names. In his famous *Lives of the Game Animals*, Ernest Thompson Seton lists other names for these animals such as prairie marmot, barking ground-squirrel, prairie barker, blacktailed prairie dog, mound yapper, yap rat, and yek-yek. Whatever the name, these were familiar animals to early visitors to the prairies. Branded as a nuisance, they have been eliminated by humans in a variety of ways. The only legally protected colony of prairie dogs in Canada is the colony on a quarter section leased by the Saskatchewan Natural History Society at Val Marie, Saskatchewan.

Once the mounds of prairie dog towns occupied hundreds of square miles. As a pioneer on the landscape, the prairie dog cannot be dismissed as a nuisance. Indeed, man is probably the first animal thus far which has the colossal conceit to arbitrarily brand as impediment, anything that gets in the path of his particular sort of earthly carnage. Mounds are the mark of a dog town. The twelve to fourteen inch (30 to 34 cm) high mounds are usually ten or twenty feet (3 or 6 m) apart in a heavily populated colony. Important in the economy of the native prairies, the prairie dogs usually formed towns in areas that were heavily grazed by bison. In such places the taller grasses were thinned from grazing and the buffalo grass and gramas were dominant. These rodents fed on annual grasses and herbs, and brought great quantities of subsoil to the surface. It may well be that the prairie dogs' overall action served to restore short grass cover, which is almost universally accepted as good food for herbivorous animals. Other beneficial action carried on by prairie dogs was the forming of burrows which enabled air to circulate underground, thereby providing oxygen for microbial functions. The deeper soil layers in turn were mixed with droppings and bits of vegetable matter. Unwittingly, the prairie dog was literally a tiller of the soil.

The burrow mounds are in themselves an interesting feature. The raised mound helps prevent flooding during violent rainstorms. As if this factor of instinctive engineering was not in itself significant, the main burrow tunnel goes downward for approximately ten feet (3 m) and lateral passages in some instances turn upward, thereby providing a pocket of air in the event that the rest of the burrow becomes filled with water.

According to Seton, when these animals were abundant, they might average twenty-five to the acre (62.5 per ha) which would mean 4,000 to every 160 acres (64 ha). Poisons ultimately swung the tide of battle, but have perhaps swung it too heavily, for now there are only a few scattered colonies in North America. The decline of this species in turn has led to the reduction of some of their natural predators to the extent that the black-footed ferret, and the Northern Kit-fox are both on the list of endangered species.

Seton referred to the prairie dogs as "Earth Spirit of the Shining Plains." Perhaps we are very busy, but, as we follow the god of speed in the daily chase of the elusive almighty dollar, we ought to remember to be sure to spare a bit of the land for the many kindred creatures that share our spaceship earth. Someday we might find that they are more important than we used to think.

25 When Love Takes the Lead

Inasmuch as "necessity" is reputed to be "the mother of invention," we now face such necessity in this world, that we are beginning to see the emergence of something that wise men have sought for many years—a land ethic!

Like most things though, our forthcoming land ethic has not grown out of the thoughts of a single generation. The idea is quite ancient, as William Lecky points out in *The History of European Morals*. He described Plutarch, who lived between 46 and 120 A.D., as placing "the duty of kindness to animals on the broad grounds of the affections....and asserts in the strongest language that every man has duties to the animal world as truly as to his fellow-man."

St. Francis of Assisi, in the 8th century, recognized the brotherhood of all life, and spoke of "Brother Wind, Sister Moon and Stars, and Sister-Mother Earth." Before Francis, there was Benedict of Nursia, founder of the Benedictine Order of Monks, who told those he invited into his order, "Believe me, upon my own experience, you will find more in the woods than in books; the forests and rocks will teach you what you cannot learn of the greatest masters." He used to say that he never had any other master in his study of the Holy Scriptures than the oaks and the beeches of the forest.

Closer to our time, Thoreau commented on the stultifying nature of our indoor education, asking himself, "What does education often do?" and answering, "It makes a straight-cut ditch of a free, meandering brook." In thinking of human relationship to the wild land, he observed, "How base are the motives that commonly carry men into the

wilderness. They have no more love for wild nature than wood sawyers have for forests. For one that comes to sketch or sing, a thousand come with ax or rifle."

In the late 19th century, George Perkins Marsh, was reminding us that we have forgotten that the earth was given us to use, rather than to destroy, or exploit for profligate waste. He called for restoration of the forests to their normal proportion, and spoke of maintaining the permanent relation of the forest to "the fields, the meadows, and the pastures, to the rain and the dews of heaven, to the springs and rivulets with which it waters the earth." Earlier he had cited the rapid devastation of the forests of eastern North America.

In 1910, Gifford Pinchot, was calling attention to the fact that North America was annually losing 400 million tons of its finest topsoil from the basin of the Mississippi River alone. He pointed to streams less navigable than formerly and said, "The soil lost by erosion from the farms and the forested mountainsides is the chief reason."

By 1915, Theodore Roosevelt advised people of his nation that, "trees must not be cut down more rapidly than they are replaced: We have taken forward steps in learning that wild beasts and birds are by right, not the property merely of the people alive today, but the property of the unborn generations whose belongings we have no right to squander; and there are even faint signs of our growing to understand that wild flowers should be enjoyed unplucked where they grow."

Aldo Leopold explained to his students that, "we abuse land because we regard it as a commodity belonging to us. When we see land as a community to which we belong, we may begin to use it with love and respect."

In 1954, Lewis Mumford was writing that we need approach both earth and man in a spirit of love, and told us: "Only when love takes the lead will the earth, and life on earth, be safe again. And not until then."

And in 1962, John F. Kennedy told his Congress that, "conservation is the highest form of national thrift."

Truly, if there is time, we are moving in the direction of an ethical attitude toward our earth. Perhaps the most subtle expression of this awareness is expressed by Albert Schweitzer in his book, *The Philosophy of Civilization*, wherein he says: "What does reverence for life say about the relations between man and the animal world? Wherever I injure life of any sort, I must be quite clear whether it is necessary. Beyond the unavoidable, I must never go; not even with what seems insignificant." He points out that the farmer who cuts hay to provide his livestock with food in winter is entitled to do so by reason of necessity. But, the same farmer, returning after his day's work, must not strike off the head of a single flower along the roadside in a casual manner. To destroy life wantonly or idly is to commit a wrong against life.

There is hope! Our awareness is growing, but the earth needs more help!

26 Clutter

Today I trudged through a foot of snow along a woodland trail. Large flakes of snow were wafting downward across my path. A hush seemed to lay over the entire land. No sound was to be heard.

How strange, I thought to myself, that humans lead such complex lives; seek to own so many things, and at the same time long for peace. Peace exists in simplicity, in the natural things of life, and when we turn away from them, it eludes us.

As I wandered along, I thought of the fact that the radio this morning was reminding people that few shopping days are left before Christmas. Commercial enterprises were informing humans that happiness is anything from a new diamond ring, to a dishwasher, or a new snowmobile beneath the Christmas tree. Happiness, I realize is none of these things—as a matter of fact, the more things with which we clutter up our lives, the less chance there is of finding happiness.

Consider how we are burdened with things. We spend our lives working in order to accumulate unwieldy furniture, and all sorts of gadgets and knick-knacks. We stumble over these things in our homes, and can't leave the house without locking the doors for fear that our hoard of treasures will be preempted by someone else. When summer comes, we load all sorts of items into cars or trucks to go off on a summer vacation, often hesitating to go very far from the vehicle because of all the treasures it contains. In the meantime, we occasionally stop to worry about whether or not we locked the basement door before we left home.

Of course, a certain number of things are reasonably necessary in order to live comfortably. But, the ability to discriminate between what is necessary and what is not necessary seems to have eluded us. How many people do you know personally, whose basements, attics, and garages are cluttered up with things they will never use, but don't have the moral fiber to give or throw away? Perhaps you are one of them. But, Christmas being what it is, everyone will buy someone else something he or she doesn't really need, and each of us, in turn, will receive things that we will put into drawers, closets, or basements—where they won't be in the way.

There is a certain paradox to this matter of possessions. While we need certain things, once we get beyond some indistinguishable point, we become burdened down with what we own. As Bertrand Russell commented, "It is preoccupation with possession, more than anything else, that prevents man from living freely and nobly."

It is very likely that we go through stages in life. When we are young, we look avidly at various things and want them. As we get older, we realize that intangible possessions—things such as health, character, experience and wisdom—are of far more importance than rooms full of inert items we own. It is sadness indeed to see people so taken up with material items that their lives are spent accumulating things that their relatives will have to sift through and argue over when they have passed on, possibly to a more meaningful sort of life.

I asked myself, "What do I want for Christmas?" Looking around at the beautiful forest, absorbing its winter coat of life-giving snow—I realized that there are two things I want. One is that I want—always—the ability to appreciate the beauty of a world whose creation was a marvel we should never cease to contemplate. The second thing I want—or hope for—is to see humanity begin to appreciate the splendor and majesty of the natural world—to see humanity reach a point whereat it no longer despoils without remorse, but begins to realize its duty of living with loving concern for the earth.

27 Twilight Time

I stood among trees, looking across a beaver pond to where a whitetail deer browsed and grazed along the opposite edge. My dog sat so close she touched my leg, as with ears cocked and nose testing the air, she watched the deer. The descending song of a veery came from a clump of willows, and in taller trees a few thrushes sang melodiously. The deer, I am sure, was aware of us, although it paid little attention. After all, the pond was between us, and dense cover just a few feet away. Besides, thickening twilight was making a more effective curtain between us with each passing moment.

In many ways it was a scene of reverence. There was a winged choir aloft in the trees, singing "Benedicite" to the day. The rumble of the creek made a peal of organ music. Good enough as a giver of sermons were the twin peaks of the mountain visible against a still, somewhat blue sky. "The mountain is in the pulpit," I mused, "and the sermon is serenity and gathering twilight. How far we go afield in search of peace, when it is all around us the moment we reflect upon it—at least in the outdoor world, if not in the busy cities."

A bat fluttered around my head—one of nature's useful, non-polluting, insect-control agents. Taken in perspective, we can live easily enough among insects, since people made it as far as the 20th century without all the insect-repellents we now feel a necessity.

Meanwhile, my dog, who had been sniffing studiously, had gone to sleep with her head on my foot. I suppose, in such a manner, she trusted herself to sleep, knowing that I couldn't leave without awakening her. Yet, I knew her sleep was such that the slightest rustling of branches or crackling brush would bring her fully awake.

A downslope convection breeze suddenly started blowing, as the upland areas cooled more rapidly than the valley. The sound of the creek was thus changed to a sharper, more staccato roar. The few mosquitoes dissipated with the breeze, and the moist smell of upslope spruces permeated the air.

"It takes time to appreciate," I thought. As Thoreau wrote, "I went to the woods because I wished to live deliberately, to front only the essential facts of life, and see if I could not learn what it had to teach, and not, when I came to die, discover that I had not lived.... Our life is frittered away by detail, simplify, simplify." In his journal, in September 1850, he made the following observation: "I saw a delicate flower had grown up two feet high between the horses' feet and the wheel track. An inch more to the right or left had sealed its fate, or an inch higher. Yet it lived to flourish, and never knew the danger it incurred. It did not borrow trouble, nor invite an evil fate by apprehending it."

The darkening world of the woods in which I sat was, and is, a friendly world. There nature goes about the business of growth and development. Who can say that we do not need such a natural environment for our own growth?

Sitting quietly in the forest in gathering dusk may not seem to be a monumental undertaking—yet it can nonetheless lead to the unrecognized, monumental understanding that all the bounty of nature, all the beauty possible in the world—is the largesse of order beyond our present comprehension.

One becomes aware that if humanity is ever to comprehend the hymn of the Universe, it must first slow its blinding pace, and uncover its muted senses. In the old Chronicle of Battel Abbey, the wise observation was made, "Man proposes, but God disposes." We must realize that when what is proposed is glib or insincere, disposal can hardly be to our advantage. We need comprehension of nature and its unwritten scrolls, more than ever—for nature is the harmony, and at present it is mankind that is out of tune. Upon reflection one can understand that humankind is exploiting (and destroying) nature for its own ends but is destroying the foundation of its own existence at an even more rapid rate. Thus humankind may disappear through its own machinations, but the Earth will endure.

28 A Handful of Miracles

One thing in favor of living somewhat close to nature is that it affords an opportunity for experiences that have become rare. One learns that the real world is not the world defined by the industrial and commercial juggernaut. It is not a plastic and steel, man-made world but an intricate and vibrant, living world of which we are but a part. It is a complex creation that made us a reality. Our future shrinks as we foolishly hack away at the foundation of our existence.

One morning I stood watching a beetle of the family Cerambycidea. Reluctantly, I will admit that such a name is a tongue twister and hardly apt to become as familiar as the names of some of the contemporary rock groups. But these beetles, vernacularly known as longhorn beetles, are of considerable economic importance. Their larvae are bore in the cambium layer or through the heartwood of various species of trees. Inasmuch as we have decided that our society is to be oriented toward the strange phenomenon known as money, we have little appreciation for such organisms as beetles that cost us money while in the quest of their daily food.

Nonetheless, the longhorn beetle I looked at this morning is a miraculous testimony to the intricate construction that exists in every tiny area of this strange living phenomenon we call nature. The beetle was about an inch long (2 1/2 cm), and befitting its name, its antennae, held nearly perpendicular to the body, were each a bit longer than the body itself.

What most impressed me about the particular individual I was observing was that it was a bit frustrated. I had several times placed a small piece of wood in front of it so that I might continue to observe it. I had been personally unaware that this particular kind of beetle was apt to vocalize, but it was making strange churring noises, perhaps in

73

anger and perhaps (as some would contend) because this was the mechanical sort of response that such an unthinking creature would make to the situation it faced.

I watched its mobile antennae being moved in various directions to detect the sort of problem confronting it, and I marvelled that such a tiny organism, compared to me, could be a master of intricate functions of motion, observation, and perhaps even of emotion.

Needless to say, I did not continue to bother the beetle for long, but allowed it to move off on its appointed rounds. Nevertheless, as I stood over this insect, a veritable giant and a nearly omnipotent power to it, I was reminded of the greater power and intelligence that stands over us, and of how uncomprehending our behavior must seem to it.

How many countless lives, I wondered, lay on the forest floor and in the litter beneath its surface. Thousands upon thousands of species, with purposes far more intricate than we even begin to realize, make up this vast complexity of the living earth. How true it is that instead of venturing into the space beyond this planet, we need to venture into understanding of the countless gaps in our knowledge of what lives and interacts on our earth.

What change would we find in our thinking if we each lived a day in simple observation of the life around us. We have national holidays and days for noting events of all sorts, but have not yet come to the point of designating a national, "Be Aware Day." Imagine having a day a year upon which we arose early and walked abroad to appreciate the magic of the earth upon which we live. In a jaded age when we think that the only miracles are the miracles we develop, we perhaps need a day to remind ourselves that daily miracles are taking place all around us. What farmer holding a handful of seed stops to realize that he is holding a handful of miracles? While many decry the existence of miracles, consider that a hundred Sequoia seeds can nestle in a teaspoon, but a single such seed produced the giant General Sherman tree that is estimated to weigh 1,250 tons, is 105 feet (32 m) in circumference at the base and is still growing!

Spring may be fading and summer approaching with the promise of fall and winter behind, but the seeds will fill and growth be stored to welcome the beneficent rays of another spring's warming sun. If we could sincerely appreciate the sustenance provided by our earth—even for a single day—might we not be better able to come to grips with the reality of the world in which we live?

29 Woodpile to Woodshed Thoughts

The seasons exert their own compulsions. The white flowers of queen's cup dropped their petals weeks ago, and now each of these miniature woodland lilies bears the single, shiny-blue berry that will ensure propagation of the species. So it is with the red berries on the Devil's club, and the bright-orange bunchberries.

Even if I had no calendar, the berries remind me that my spare time should be spent carrying armloads of wood to the woodshed and stacking them. The wood has been stacked outside long enough to be fully dried. If the berries are not reminder enough, the pine cone a red squirrel dropped on my head the other morning, should certainly advise me that harvest season is at hand.

As a consequence of all the good advice I receive from my environment, I spend a part of each day carrying wood. Undoubtedly I could arrange some mechanical contrivance to make my work less arduous—but if I did so, I would be depriving myself of both the pleasure and the exercise that I receive with my annual wood supply. Of course, it is one of the simpler secrets of life, to enjoy the things you do. After having cut all the wood, I find it a great pleasure to watch the wealth of winter warmth accumulate under the woodshed roof—safe from the freezing storms and the 200 inches of snow that may fall in this part of the mountain valley.

"It's strange," I muse, as I wend my way from woodpile to woodshed. "If I think of my winter fuel in terms of its monetary wealth, it is worth many more of those things called dollars than it was last year.

Yet, it is about the same amount of wood, and will produce about the same amount of heat."

"Strange indeed!" I think to myself. "I wonder if the squirrels have been told that their pine cones are worth more this year—come to think of it, I had perhaps better not say anything, or perchance the pine trees will hear, and possibly go on strike for higher wages, or greater fringe benefits."

"On second thought though, I'll say nothing anyway, because I don't believe the squirrels would be interested. Quite likely they would understand that inflation is some sort of virus specific only to an overpopulation of the synthetic wealth people call money."

Unreal these thoughts may seem; but no more unreal perhaps than the strange system to which we have tied our economic hopes. Farmers will perhaps understand me well. To the squirrel, the pine cone would be a more realistic basis for wealth than some shiny metal stolen from one hole in the earth, and buried covetously in another. Similarly, the loaf of bread, the pound of wheat, or the cord of firewood are realistic symbols of wealth. Possibly, since they do not lend themselves well to hoarding (since storage would become a problem), those who originally intended to accumulate nearly endless wealth for themselves, somehow deluded their compatriots as to the real nature of wealth. One would only have to ask a starving man if he preferred a loaf of bread or a bar of gold; or ask a freezing man if he preferred gold to firewood—to know the real nature of wealth. Need it be added, that one could ask a sick person whether she preferred gold or health; and we would have pretty well summed up the difference between the things we assume are important, and the things that are really important. Meditating along these lines, one can quickly come to the conclusion that if we had even a modicum of intelligence, we would waste no time beating our metallic military might into plowshares and pruning hooks—and would then tend the land with the love it deserves but has never received.

In truth, we live in a world wherein many have eyes and do not see; many have ears to hear, but do not understand; and many have tongues that twist and turn but consistently evade truth.

Such may be only "woodpile to woodshed truths," or "pine cone to squirrels' nest truths," and may be too simple for a sophisticated society—unless we remember that sophistry, by definition, is "deceptively subtle reasoning," and that we all need to be as children again, if we are to recognize reality in the synthetic garments wrought for her by the clacking looms of a society estranged from the natural world.

30 The Law of Parsimony

It is peaceful here in the woods. No traffic has been along the road for several hours. The gas lamp hisses quietly on the wall, and wood crackles in the heater. The dog rests companionably beside me, with her head on my foot. I think she sleeps more soundly that way because she knows that I can't move without disturbing her.

I ponder. Perhaps this sort of atmosphere is conducive to sorting over ideas and trying to come to conclusions. One of the difficulties involved in arriving at any sort of conclusion is the nagging doubt, "Am I right?"

Years ago I was in a philosophy class in which the law of parsimony was introduced. This law, sometimes called Occam's Razor, simply states, "Entities should not be multiplied beyond necessity." At the time, it seemed like a valid principle. It served to remind us that we should never consider more than the necessary facts when we seek to arrive at conclusions.

For a long while I thought that the law of parsimony was a principle one should always seek to utilize. Later I became aware of the immense complexity of nature, and of the unavoidable truth that in nature, "There are no isolated incidents—everything affects everything else." It was evident that one might arrive at a solution to some technological problems by employing the law of parsimony; but if he or she wanted to consider a problem in the light of its entire effect on and within the natural world, no such approach would be possible. I began to realize that hasty decisions can produce long-range disasters, and that one can never proceed more rapidly than nature itself. In effect, this would mean that the limitation on progress would be much more thorough awareness than we now possess.

As I contemplate this matter, I become more and more convinced that our entire educational system is founded on a hopeless premise. Instead of basing the educational program on a strong understanding of the natural world, and using that as a platform for human endeavour; we have instead built the educational structure on an assumption that human culture is of a loftier status than nature itself. Such an assumption increasingly seems to be proving itself a fatal mistake.

Periodically I need to consider the whole matter in the context of modern times. I realize that I am lumped in a category that is reserved for people who are classified as environmental radicals. This is to be expected in a world that functions without conscience. At best though, such people can only be considered as very weak brakes on a runaway train. The train is running full speed toward some station named "Progress," but the engineers don't seem to realize that the tracks are laid in quicksand.

Appraising human endeavor, and human analysis of progress, from out here in the woods, I can understand that there is a reason for the great "busy-ness" assumed by the world's people. It is that we utilize the "busy-ness" in order to rationalize away the necessity of pausing to evaluate what we are doing. Over a hundred years ago, Thoreau saw the same thing beginning to happen, and chided his readers: "Pause, Avast! Why so seeming fast and deadly slow?" Imagine being too busy to think about anything but making a living—at that not even to do any living, but just to make a living! Imagine being too busy to think about poisoning the air we breathe, the water we drink, the soil that grows our food! Imagine being too busy to think about eroding away the hillsides and valley bottoms that will raise the food for the future generations we profess to love!

Part of the problem is that we have already educated ourselves into the pattern we now follow; and since there is always a strong natural desire to justify what we are doing, we are attempting to impose the status quo as the be-all and end-all of life. At that, it may be the end-all! We gloss over the evidence that our way of life is wrong, and perhaps assume we can appeal to a higher court, if the natural world declares us "misfits." We may labor under the delusion that the human species has inherited the earth and can make its own laws, but there are no sacrosanct species on this planet.

It would perhaps be remiss to ignore the changing trend, and the small effort that is being made to restore natural landscapes and natural

79

balances. Upon sober thought, though, we would not expect a banker to be highly impressed if we deposited a few pennies now and then, while we continued overdrawing our accounts by hundreds or thousands of dollars. We make a mighty show of dedicating a few "natural areas" or "provincial parks" as though such deeds will make up for thunderous abuse of the earth. The books will not balance with such shoddy logic.

We are still playing with the law of parsimony—still considering the minimum number of factors needed to attain gluttonous ends. Like Thoreau's miser looking for "a post-hole in the middle of Paradise," totally oblivious to "the angels going to and fro," we exhaust the resources of this earthly steed that carries us to some distant rendezvous in the heavens. What sort of revelation will it take to awaken us?

31 The Great Spirit and the Grizzly

Bears still hold a mysterious fascination for humans. Attitudes vary of course. To some, the sight of a bear is the instant signal for the word "trophy" to enter the thoughts. Some think of observing and photographing bears, and there are some who merely think they would rather be someplace else, preferably far away.

To the North American Indians, bears had a special significance. In the eastern part of the continent, bears were referred to as "cousins." The Tete de Boule of Quebec referred to bears as "Grandfather." Other tribes called them the "chief's sons" or "old man." Among the Crees of the plains, they were "four-legged humans." The grizzly in particular was called the "old man in a furred cloak" by some tribes.

One of the strangest stories I think, is the story of creation handed down among the Shasta and Modoc Indians of the United States:

When the Great Spirit came to earth, he made the earth blossom with great beauty. The forests and fields, the verdant meadows, the flowing streams were part of his work. The birds of the air, the fishes and the animals came to be. And chief among the animals was the magnificent grizzly bear. But this animal was different than it is today, for even though possessed of heavy fur, strong teeth and tremendous claws, the grizzlies of that time walked on two feet, carried heavy clubs for weapons, and talked among themselves in a language of their own.

One day the youngest and most beautiful daughter of the Great Spirit wandered away from the tepee. She lost her way, and in due time became tired and lay down to sleep. A father grizzly returning from the

hunt with an elk under his arm, saw the beautiful girl and took her home to his wife. She was adopted into the family and grew up among them. In due time, when the son of this family was old enough to marry, he was betrothed to the daughter of the Great Spirit. Their children, blood of the grizzly bears and the Great Spirit, became the Indian tribes.

The legend continues: When the mother grizzly was aged and about to die, she became repentant and sent her son to tell the Great Spirit what had happened to his daughter. At first he was so happy and excited that he raced down the mountain to find his daughter, his tracks still showing plainly on the mountainside. But when he neared the place where the grizzly bears were assembled and waiting for him, he became enraged; for the bears had dared to bring forth a new race on earth. His glare caused the old mother grizzly to fall down dead and the other grizzlies howled in protest.

He became even more irate and ordered the grizzlies to drop their clubs and never use them again. He took away their power of speech and ordered them down onto all four legs. He picked up his daughter to bear her back to Mt. Shasta and ordered her children, the Indians, to disperse into the world.

Thus it was that the Indians were created and thus it was that the grizzly bears have had to resort to the life of tooth and claw that is the life of most other animals.

As has been pointed out by the Modoc and Shasta tribes, one has but to look at grizzly bears to know that they once stood erect, for their arms are much shorter than their legs; the soles of their feet are like our own; they walk flat-footed, and have no tails. And when their honor is at stake, they rise upon their hind legs.

Roger Pocock pointed out, "Bears yearn to man.... Their sentiments get mixed, they act confused and naturally if they're shot at they'll get hostile, same as you and me. They is misunderstood and that's how nobody has a kind word for grizzlies."

Or to put it another way, Ralph Waldo Emerson once commented: "To be great is to be misunderstood." Bears fit this category nicely.

33 Sober Eyes

When I observed my nine-year-old son busily scraping out a miniature foundation, anchoring six-inch-high sidewalls and then finishing his edifice with a scrap of plywood for a roof, I asked him why he was building the house. "Oh, for a wild animal," he said. "Do you think one will move in?" I asked him. "Oh yes," he replied with the faith of youth. I promptly forgot about it, but he did not, and two weeks later he came racing to tell us that he wanted to show us something. He took the lid off his mansion, and within, blinking owlishly, (would "toadishly" be better?) was a large toad, who had found a subterranean passageway beneath the foundation. The toad was, after much reflection, named Sober-Eyes, and has been quite content with his residence. He may be found within his home each day and is now quite used to the roof being removed and to being watched by a freckle-faced young lad. What he thinks about it all, I am not sure, because toads don't tell, but apparently there is some mystic trust passing between his amphibian world and that of his home builder.

Actually we look upon Sober-Eyes as an excellent neighbor. After all, his residence is only about ten yards from the garden, and I am sure that his nightly forays include a lot of insect control. I recall reading years ago that a toad was worth about thirty dollars a year as an insect eater, and at today's inflated prices, his value would be well over twice that amount. From now until cool weather comes and Sober-Eyes digs himself down a few inches beneath the woodland litter, his chief interest in life will be eating, and that means that his stomach will be filled with insects, mites, small spiders, and whatever else appears edible. According to one textbook on Amphibia, his stomach will be filled to capacity about four times in each twenty-four hour period.

Toads are remarkably well distributed throughout the world. One would normally think that they would be found only in quite warm locations and at lower elevations, but they are found in the Himalayas at an altitude of 14,000 feet (4,267 m), and have been collected in Tibet at 16,000 feet (4,876 m). Although it would perhaps be assumed that their life span would be brief, European toads have been known to live as long as thirty-six years, and it is quite possible that Sober-Eyes is older than the nine-year-old boy who is his self-appointed guardian. Toads have many enemies, including snakes, hawks, owls, weasels, and highways (not to mention acid rain); but their tendency to immobility and the acrid secretion of their skin may enable them to be lucky enough to survive for a long period of time. Although their intelligence level has been studied and found to be quite modest, studies have also indicated that they learn from experience and since experience can favor survival, the chance of living longer may increase with each succeeding day...up to a point of course.

Each year, early in spring, toads congregate in ponds for reproductive purposes. I recall taking a color slide some years ago of a toad hopping over a snowy patch on his way to a pond a few yards away. The eggs are laid in long strings rather than in clusters as are the eggs of frogs.

At night toads are wanderers. Although their diet is varied, it has been found experimentally that some obnoxious insects are avoided. It was noted that a toad would attempt to disgorge a stinkbug, and after a single experience would learn to avoid that species of insect. Some observations have indicated that certain toads have a marked fondness for ants of one particular species.

Wherever he goes on his nightly forays, we hope that Sober-Eyes will be careful. Our young fellow told us that as long as Sober-Eyes will use his home it will be kept there for him. Let's hope that years from now we can look upon him as an old settler.

34 Breaking the Machine Habit

Havelock Ellis once wrote that "the greatest task before civilization at present is to make machines what they ought to be, the slaves, instead of the masters of men."

Perhaps we haven't really noticed it, but we have become the slaves of machines in ever so many ways, some of them quite subtle. We have but to consider the telephone to realize the truth of our enslavement to one single machine. Let the telephone ring, and ever so many people dutifully leave their meals, their favorite recreation, their bath, or their bed to answer it. Usually, as most of us freely admit, the incoming call is hardly worth receiving, let alone leaving what one was doing.

In ever so many ways, we are shackled to the machines that we fancy are our servants. With a few idle moments on hand, rather than plunge into new frontiers of thought or indulge in silent reflection, we automatically turn the television on, and often dispiritedly sit before it as partially unwilling captives of the ephemeral characters dancing on the screen.

In similar manner, though we think about it only sketchily, our efficient modern transportation has forced mobility on us. Knowing that we can go, whether it be to Hawaii, New Zealand, or merely across the continent, we have a built-in restlessness, a sort of nagging feeling that we should go somewhere, anywhere, as long as we are on the move. Properly used mobility is an advantage. When discontent is fostered merely by knowing that we can go somewhere, then we are the slaves of the machines in question.

Lana/94.

Ideas about machines have changed over the years. Albert Schweitzer tells an interesting story about one attitude toward machines. He speaks of the writings of Chawng-tse in which he refers to a pupil of Confucius' who saw a gardener repeatedly going to a stream to bring water to his flower bed. The pupil asked if he would not like to lessen his labor by fashioning a draw well. When asked by the gardener how that might be done he explained how a long piece of wood, light at one end and heavy at the other, could be used to lever pails of water out of the stream with minimum effort. The gardener pondered this idea and then replied: "I have heard my teacher say: 'If a man uses machines, he carries on all the affairs of life like a machine; whoever carries on his affairs like a machine gets a machine-like heart; and when anyone has a machine-like heart in his breast, he loses true simplicity.'"

Schweitzer goes on to say that the very dangers foreseen by the gardener are now rampant among us today. He observes that as a result of the machine revolution we often live depressing, monotonous, materialistic lives, unrelieved by any close relationship with nature.

Whether or not we realize it, the environmental crisis in which we live, is closely related to machines and to the fantastic energy they gobble up as their daily bread. Studies have indicated that the energy demand made by modern humans is the equivalent of a population of 11 billion people in Canada alone. Each human is propped up by some 550 mechanical servants, this figure being based on the amount of energy used in Canada, divided by a population of about 22 million people at the time the computations were made. The energy servants exist in the form of such things as the motors in automobiles, refrigerators, vacuum cleaners, freezers, fans, blenders, hair dryers, cassette decks, etc.

The relationship between machines and humans becomes a bit silly when one realizes that the BTU's of energy required by farm machinery and farming techniques in Canada actually exceed the BTU's of food produced as a result of the modern farming process. We use a greater amount of fossil fuel energy in farm machinery than we receive in food fuel energy. Obviously something is missing from the glorious fairy stories we hear about our energy efficient society. We have actually developed far more energy than we can use efficiently and the problem today is not further development, but economical use of energy already developed.

The problem of the machine-human relationship has actually become a problem of whether or not all society is simply turning into an enormous inefficient monster that is strangling individuality and uniqueness among humans. As statistical data accumulates about humans, there is a great tendency to oversimplify the very factor of individuality that makes a person truly human. People in their unwitting willingness to abet the cult of efficiency only bring the day closer when the machine ceases to merely dominate society and actually begins to run it totally.

Fortunately for that which is latently human in most of us, the real world continues to exist in spite of society's drive toward the mechanical state and the advent of total mechanical man. There is much evidence to suggest that the stress of living mechanically is beginning to tell, and is beginning to promote a breakaway response on the part of many people. The determined effort by these people to return to a life of simplicity is a crack extending all the way to the centre of the mechanical pipe dreams. With humanity's habitual reluctance to move before a total crisis asserts itself, we still worship at the temple of the machine, although our worship is fraught with a growing realization that the machine has been every bit as demanding as the other gods man has fashioned for himself.

Lewis Mumford points out that simplicity does not avoid mechanical aids, but merely seeks to avoid being victimized by them. He advises what might seem like radical behavior, until one realizes that it enables a return to more conscious forms of self-directed behavior. "This holds for the whole routine of life; never to use mechanical power when human muscles can conveniently do the work, never to use a motor car where one might easily walk, never to acquire information or knowledge except for the satisfaction of some immediate or prospective want." (Here he is referring to the accumulation of useless data in our computer systems and filing cabinets throughout the world). He points out that each time we choose a non-mechanical alternative, we thereby emancipate ourselves, if only a tiny bit, from those forces that would enslave us into total mechanical dependence.

Breaking the machine habit, we will find, is every bit as difficult as disposing of any other addiction.

34 The World Is Too Much with Us

Sometimes I believe that humanity cheerfully indulges itself in depression. In the last few weeks I have received a number of letters from various individuals I know. Perhaps it is a dragging-winter syndrome, with people feeling that spring is far behind schedule. At any rate, the tone of the various letters was something one might expect after three weeks of foggy drizzle.

We have a tendency to expect too much. We often believe that the world should cast sunbeams onto our paths without any particular effort on our own parts.

As you probably know, it doesn't work that way.

We do live in a rather tightly circumscribed world. The center of that world is the elusive, intangible portion we call the self. We have a single window on the world, and that is through the impressions the self can gain by looking at the world with its unique viewpoint. No one else sees the world in quite the same manner.

If we really stop and think about things, one of the sanest ways to live is to expect quite little from life. This does not mean, that we would not try to achieve things, nor does it mean that we would resign ourselves to misery. It simply means that we could see the good in what happens much more clearly if false or unreasonable expectations are not held. To be grateful for whatever good occurs, and to accept those things which are not pleasing—but which we have no power to change—is the secret of leading a relatively peaceful life.

Confucius once observed that, "Humility is the solid foundation of all the virtues." The traditional Chinese custom of feeling honored by relatively small blessings is a wise step in having an ordered personality.

Life in our quite materialistic world has interfered with our ability to measure values. We live with the sensational to such a great extent that we expect our pleasure to be vivid. Life must be in technicolor. The chuckle is not sufficient. We must have the belly laugh to be satisfied. What it adds up to is that we have experienced such dulling of the senses by Madison Avenue lifestyles, that we can only comprehend glittering joy or exhausting depression.

The poet William Wordsworth recognized the same sort of problem in his own times. "The world is too much with us, late and soon,"

he wrote. "Getting and spending, we lay waste our powers: Little we see in Nature, that is ours." Nothing has changed if we think of it. We still concentrate much of our energy on "getting and spending," and we know so little about the natural world that we still cannot comprehend our place in it.

Probably the very first step in relieving oneself of the foggy drizzle blues is to try to remove all vestiges of hypocrisy from life. Ever so many people claim that they must act as hypocrites in order to keep jobs, must have a business personality or a corporate personality just to survive. But that is death in life.

It may be one of the peculiarities of the universe that each of us is different, and this fact is part of an immense plan we cannot even begin to conceive. The purpose of life is not business at all, but is life itself. If we permit ourselves to be ground to ciphers because a job says we must, then we are better off scrounging a mere subsistence living than we are rolling in velvet while we destroy "the very talent that it is death to hide."

The truth of the matter is that many jobs are quite worthless, quite meaningless, and many people in those very jobs admit that fact freely when they are in company they can trust. How many people today are engaged in total vacuum jobs, making meaningless doodles with computers in designated squares, professing a sales pitch they do not believe, or creating a product they know is intrinsically worthless, destructive, or inimical to civilization?

On paper these people might be called successes, but in their hearts they know they are miserable. The strangeness at the root of it all, is that these people have often sold their own integrity in order to maintain a facade of achievement.

So what happens? Do people in such positions, often at odds with themselves, cry out, "Stop the world, I want to get off?" Do they become revolutionaries, anarchists, or adopt one of the superfluous "isms" with which the world is cluttered?

The answer, as I see it, is complex. It is a sort of "No, but Yes." They do not become negativists in a destructive sense. First they make peace with themselves, and then if you would have a name for it, they attempt to become reformers in whatever way possible. Perhaps we might say they try to open the dusty closets of thought and attempt to let some light into the dark corners since our most prevalent affliction, brain rot, cannot stand exposure to sunlight and cleansing air.

Actually the line of Wordsworth's is evidence of what might be done. Getting and spending must become a minor part of life. After all, the less one needs the richer one is. Along with that new posture toward life, there might be a more intensive search into the nature of oneself, and into the deep insights offered by the world around us—the natural world. If Blake could recognize a world in a grain of sand, heaven in a wild flower, and hold infinity in the palm of his hand, then all of us might be able to see enough to cause the foggy drizzle to disband and the sun to shine.

35 Nonviolence

Life is not all problems and no answers. It's just that the problems are obvious and the answers quite obscure. We often tend to need exotic foods and strong drink because we suffer from too bland intake for our minds. That's not to say, though, that there aren't fascinating things to think about if we look into the less evident corners of life where the bright lights of Madison Avenue are not focused.

Hitting the nail rather bluntly, Thomas Merton made a brief observation about the central issue we all face. He said it quite simply: "It is a crisis of sanity first of all. The problems of the nations are the problems of mentally-deranged people, but magnified a thousand times because they have the full, straight-faced approbation of a schizoid society, schizoid national structures, schizoid military and business complexes, and need one add, schizoid religious sects."

Another analyst, Ananda Coomaraswamy, sees us economically determined as a society, to keep on going, we "know not where, and we call this rudderless voyage Progress." Coomaraswamy feels we are, "at war with ourselves and therefore at war with one another. Western man is unbalanced and the question: Can he recover himself? is a very real one."

Part of the answer may lie in the meanings of two words, "satyagraha" and "ahimsa," and the man responsible for the importance of these words is Mohandus K. Gandhi.

By and large we have very little idea of the political and spiritual importance of Gandhi's life. Gandhi receives typical superficial treatment in our modern social studies programs, and is somehow vaguely identified in most people's minds as a person who had something to do with the independence of India, and something to do, in a sort of uncomprehending way, with a concept we call nonviolence. With our North American reverence for beef, brawn and Wheaties heroes, we are a bit fuzzy on things that have to do with people in the teeming, doomed-in-our-minds portion of the world we call Asia.

It would be possible to spend many pages discussing satyagraha and ahimsa, and arguing their merits, but I will use this space to describe them briefly and hope that you will investigate them out of your own interest.

Satyagraha refers to truth, as a matter of fact, to the very spirit of truth. When we say in a generalized fashion that, "Honesty is the best policy," we are only on the fringes of satyagraha. Sometimes, as most of us know, truth can become the worst policy we can follow if we want to be successful in the human world of endeavor. But the idea of satyagraha is such that it is the essence of truth itself, and even though it may be supremely unprofitable, if one can comprehend it, it needs to be followed wherever it leads. Thomas Aquinas, in his *Summa*, refers to an intellectual principle or intellectual vision in all humans, and one must either follow it or turn away from it.

The extension of the idea of truth, leads ultimately to the idea of ahimsa, or non-violence. As Gandhi expressed it, "non-violence implies as complete self-purification as is humanly possible." In our society we tend to look upon nonviolence as a sort of "sissyfication." We give lip-service to the idea that the meek shall inherit the earth, while we worship power and violence. Yet, as Gandhi pointed out,

"The strength of nonviolence is in exact proportion to the ability of the nonviolent person to inflict violence." In other words it is more impressive for a burly, rugged individual to follow a path of nonviolence than it is for a weaker individual to do so. Just think too, what a refreshing treat it would be to the world to have a nonviolent superpower that didn't rattle its rocket muscle.

It is always worth remembering that the thoughts of any single man are undoubtedly a product of his training and exposure to ideas. Desiderius Erasmus, in the 15th century, had things to say about the whole concept of nonviolence: "If you can avoid evil by suffering it yourself, do so. Try to help your enemy by overcoming him with kindness and meekness. It is better that you be enriched with the advantage of patience than to render evil for evil. It is not enough to practice the golden rule in this matter. The greater your position the more ready you ought to be to forgive another's crime."

It is a strange thing. We live in a society that is extremely rich in ideas. To put it bluntly, we have stored up enough insights to create a true civilization on earth. Perhaps Gandhi was right when he wrote, "When the practice of 'ahimsa' becomes universal, God will reign on earth as he does in Heaven." Quoting Thomas Merton, "St. Peter looked for a limit to forgiveness. Seven times, and then the sin was irreversible! But Christ told him that forgiveness must be repeated over and over again, without end."

In a world wherein nations reel from corruption, where even petty pilfering runs into millions of dollars per day; and in a world lacking a philosophy that will calm the growing thunderclouds of military might, we could do worse than look at Gandhi's thoughts of another way to face life on our planet. We maintain a surrealistic artificiality in our false concept of the good life. Dreamlike we go through motions of dinners, teas, social activities without meaning, while the invisible hands of a cosmic clock move us nearer the inevitable outcome of the events we keep in motion. There is only incipient goodness in all of us, at best, but this flake, this tiny golden glow, is the fragment we need polish until its light enables us to see the higher path we need to follow.

Robinson's injunction to Tristam seems to fit all of us well:
Whether you will or not
You are a King, Tristam, for you are one
Of the time-tested few that leave the world,
When they are gone, not the same place it was.
Mark what you leave.

Other Hancock House Titles

Robert Service
51/2 X 81/2, 64 pp. SC
ISBN 0-88839-223-0

Robert Service
51/2 X 81/2, 64 pp. SC
ISBN 0-88839-224-9

Jack London
51/2 X 81/2, 104 pp. SC
ISBN 0-88839-259-1

Chief Dan George and
Helmut Hirnschall
51/2 X 81/2, 96 pp. SC
ISBN 0-88839-231-1

Chief Dan George and
Helmut Hirnschall
51/2 X 81/2, 96 pp. SC
ISBN 0-88839-233-8

Mike Puhallo, Brian Brannon,
and Wendy Liddle
51/2 X 81/2, 64 pp. SC
ISBN 0-88839-368-7

Robert F. Harrington
51/2 X 81/2, 96 pp. SC
ISBN 0-88839-367-9

pj johnson
51/2 X 81/2, 64 pp. SC
ISBN 0-88839-366-0

James and Susan Preyde
51/2 X 81/2, 96 pp. SC
ISBN 0-88839-362-8

All titles available from HANCOCK HOUSE PUBLISHERS, 1431 Harrison Ave., Blaine, WA 98230-5005
(604) 538-1114   Fax: (604) 538-2262   Mastercard, Visa, or Check accepted.